Be Still

KARIN LARSEN FORD

Fulton Books, Inc.
Meadville, PA

Published by Fulton Books 2021

ISBN 978-1-64952-876-6 (paperback)
ISBN 978-1-64952-877-3 (digital)

Printed in the United States of America

To my many earthly angels who lovingly came to my rescue and helped me to walk along this new path in my life.

Prologue

Once again my world was about to shift on its axis. I wasn't ready. It was early Monday morning on May 4, 2015. My husband, Robin, was driving. Heading home to Arizona on I-8, we'd barely left San Diego when my son's picture popped up on my cell phone.

"Mom, how are you doing?" John asked.

I greeted his welcome voice with a smile and proceeded to serve up a description of our weekend activities. We'd spent a long weekend on Sail Bay, where Robin attended a two-day continuing education seminar related to his psychology practice. I had come along for the ride and to spend time with our San Diego kids. John heard me out, then he shared the reason for his call. He had finished training to become a licensed pilot. He had his pilot's license. Together with a coworker John already owned an older four-passenger Cessna 172. Unbidden tears welled up. Warning bells droned in my head while he spoke. I could only listen in stunned silence. I needed time to pull myself together. Needed time to digest this unwelcome news, that apparently was already shared with the rest of the family. With John's surprise disclosure, it was as if a timer had been set, and there was absolutely nothing I could do to stop it. Something regarding lessons had come up the previous year while John and his family vacationed with us in Arizona.

"Please, don't do that, John," I'd implored.

He'd responded rather emphatically. "Mom, I *am* going to learn to fly."

Reminding myself that my son was an adult, I'd dropped the subject. *Maybe it'll never happen.* Over the years, both John and my older son, Ken, shared their ambitions to fly. My children grew up around airplanes. Aviation was in their blood. There was never a time in their childhood when flying in small private planes was not a part of their lives. However, that had all come to an abrupt halt. When John was only twelve, his father and our two youngest children perished in a tragic plane crash.

The long drive home slowly gave way to resignation. I had to admit to myself that I was proud of my son's achievement. This, in spite of the overwhelming emotion and a nearly constant flood of silent tears until we reached Yuma. John had mastered a long-held goal. And hadn't I always encouraged my children to go for their dreams? Years back I'd sent John a small square magnet with an inscription by Thoreau: "Go confidently in the direction of your dreams! Live the life you've imagined."

Over the ensuing months I came to appreciate the true passion John had for flying. It was so plainly evident in the excitement on his face when he piloted his plane. Flying had become John's dream. This was not always the case. As a young child, John was a white knuckle flyer. I wondered if my boy's passion for flying was fueled by something deeper.

Chapter 1

John and his wife, Cheryl, met just weeks after John returned from serving a two-year mission in Denmark. While skiing together in Utah, they fell in love. Soon after, Cheryl relocated from BYU to Arizona State University. On Saturday, December 19, 1992, they married in the Mesa Arizona Temple for time and for all eternity. Both graduated from ASU nursing school. Over ten years, four beautiful children were born to them.

Their first child, Max, was born in Scottsdale shortly after Cheryl graduated nursing school. My sons had long ago stated a preference for staying in Arizona, where they grew up. But plans often change. When Max was only a few months old, John and Cheryl moved their family to Sandy, Utah. They'd purchased a home within walking distance of three of Cheryl's sisters and their families. Cheryl had missed her sisters, and she missed the mountains in Utah. She insisted, we did not have *real* mountains in Phoenix, and the desert climate was too hot for her. Other moves followed in pursuit of grad school, as well as the ideal location to raise their family. They'd finally settled on five acres, high in the hills, in Grants

Pass, Oregon. Surrounded by the pine tree-covered hills of Josephine County, this was a lovely Norman Rockwell kind of town. Here is where their youngest child, Ashlynn, was born.

As nurse anesthetist, John held a well-paying job at the Medical Center in Grants Pass. He loved his profession and was chief for his anesthesia group. Yet he could not seem to put to rest his desire to go to medical school. That had been his dream since high school. Unfortunately, after grad school and with his family growing, it was pushed back. But life for them seemed pretty sweet, and it was a joy to be around them. Frequently, on some special adventure together, this good family enjoyed living to the fullest. Their two fine boys, Max and Luke, were wholesome young men. Reagan and Ashlynn, two beautiful little girls, were the apples of their father's eye. All were busy and happily engaged. Mom and Dad served diligently in church callings. Much of John's free time was spent in scouting. He loved the opportunity for outdoor activities with his two boys and their friends.

Chapter 2

Robin and I share a blended family. We have twenty-four wonderful grandchildren. Extras have happily been added along the way, as life rarely goes exactly as planned. Chloe Anne is our newest grandchild. This precious little girl was born to my son Ken and daughter-in-law Chelsea in mid-January. Anticipating the birth of their first baby kicked off 2016 as a particularly good year. Ken and Chelsea had married in our backyard on the last day of February 2015, in a beautiful garden wedding attended by eighty family and friends. Only rarely does it rain in Arizona. Yet on their wedding day, dark clouds steadily clustered overhead as guests arrived for the ceremony. Fortunately, the Rain Gods held their peace. And as if heaven itself blessed this special union, a bright shaft of sunlight enveloped the lovely couple just as they were pronounced husband and wife. Two weeks before the birth of their daughter, Ken and Chelsea were sealed in the majestic San Diego Temple "for time and for all eternity." When this new family returned home from the hospital with little Chloe Anne, my fourteen-year-old grandson Robbie greeted his stepmother with the words, "Thank you,

Chelsea, for my little sister." On the first anniversary of her parents' wedding day, Chloe was given a name and a blessing. This occasion, once again, brought our family together. Because Cheryl refused to get in John's plane, they flew into Lindbergh Field on a commercial jet. They'd left their kids behind in Grants Pass with big brother Max in charge. Almost seventeen, Max was a responsible young man. A top athlete, he was also inducted into the National Honor Society. Max played several instruments and was active in orchestra. But weeks earlier, a real live bear had paid a not-so-welcome visit to their front porch. This Grandma was going to pray really hard that the bear did not return to eat her grandchildren in their parents' absence. Ken had made arrangements for a late lunch on Harbor Island. The clear blue sky above seemingly begged us to eat outside on the patio. Directly across the bay was the impressive skyline of downtown San Diego and a clear view of the San Diego-Coronado Bridge. Below that impossibly long, tall bridge, we watched a variety of boats sail on the gentle blue waters. The illusion of large diamonds shimmered on the water, where bright sunlight played on the ripples. On this idyllic afternoon, we formalized plans to gather again for Thanksgiving, this time in Grants Pass. Already excited for this next family reunion, we were blissfully unaware, as we strolled along the waterfront while taking pictures, that our lives were about to change.

Early Sunday morning on June 19, I sent a text to our sons wishing them Happy Father's Day. John responded with a selfie. He was squinting in the bright morning sun from a balcony in Hawaii. He and Cheryl had brought their four kids to the Big Island to visit friends who had relocated from Grants Pass. Lodging at a resort, they were having a blast—it was paradise. Before flying home, they posted a picture of the six of them by the beautiful Kona Hawaii Temple in Kailua-Kona.

Only days after their return, John flew to California, where he held a part-time job at a hospital in Salinas. While working in California, he often had extra time on his hands. Over July 4 weekend, we texted back and forth about his recent visit to a pain clinic in Medford. He'd long been interested in pain medicine and was trying to get his foot in the door. Tuesday morning, on July 5, it was not yet six o'clock when I received a text from Cheryl. She wanted to know what time I was expected at the Gilbert Temple, where I serve on Tuesdays. I texted the time I needed to leave. Robin and I were halfway out the door for our customary morning walk and thinking of my already full schedule for the day, I added, "I can talk now." When I received no response, we left for our walk. She'd call when she had a minute. The kids didn't have school. Cheryl likes to sleep in, and though I was somewhat surprised by her early text, I didn't give it much thought. It was lovely outside, not yet oppressively hot. We thoroughly enjoy these early morning walks, before the Arizona summer sun heats up the air and everything within her scorching reach. The multitude of birds in our neighborhood orchestrated their loud competition of happy morning tunes—more of a cacophony, actually! Our neighborhood is surrounded by man-made lakes. Quacking ducks parade around lawns and streets. Blue herons and white egrets fish for their daily meal along water's edge. The sky was a brilliant blue. Not a single cloud in view. We glanced at each other and repeated our favorite motto, "Another beautiful day in paradise!" We hadn't gone far when my cell phone rang. It was only minutes past six, and this time I felt a familiar kick in my solar plexus. I hurried to unzip my shirt pocket to get to my phone. Ken's picture flashed before me on my cell.

"Mom, what are you doing?" Kenny sounded nearly breathless as he immediately rattled on. "Is Robin with you? Have you talked with Cheryl?" I related to him the texts she and I had exchanged.

"Mom." My firstborn son hesitated with a long sigh. "Well… I can't *not* tell you… John didn't make it home last night!"

There it was. Those ominous words took my breath away. They were like icy prongs squeezing the chambers of my heart. I couldn't think straight. My thoughts jumbled as if I'd received a hard blow to my head. It was as if my brain refused to let those fateful words sink in. Yet deep down in the depth of my soul, I already knew I would eventually hear those dreaded words. It was a matter of time. And that time had come. I sensed that Kenny knew it too. We both knew it was already over. My limbs grew heavy. Strength drained from my body. My whole being was seized by an overpowering sadness. A gaping feeling of loss—a feeling of utter helplessness consumed my soul. Somehow, I was still standing on my own two feet, still holding the phone to my ear. As if from far away I heard my son's sorrowful pleading. "Be strong again, Mom. Please be an example to our family. Mom, please, can you do it again!"

I still don't know how Robin and I walked home. There had to be angels attending us. I did not see angels. I only know we did not walk home alone. Silently we knelt to pray. My dear husband prayed that my son be protected. He prayed that John's plane would be located in a speedy manner. As I listened to my husband's voice pleading so earnestly in prayer, I saw in my mind's eye the vastness of tree-covered hills representing the Oregon landscape. There are millions and millions and millions of trees in Oregon. My son was out there. Alone! Somewhere! How would we ever find him? Robin prayed for me to be comforted. He prayed for Cheryl. Individually, he prayed for Max, for Luke, for Reagan, and for little Ashlynn. He prayed that our family would find strength and comfort while we waited for John to be brought home. My husband prayed that John would be found alive. I already knew that John would not be found alive.

In a daze I walked into our bedroom. The beige honeycomb blinds were up. The room was light and orderly. I felt pleased that I'd made the bed before we left on our early morning walk, then immediately chastised myself. *What a crazy thing to think about right now.*

My gaze shifted beyond the slope of our green lawn to the ripples on the lake. It was such a lovely view through the hanging branches of the large sissoo trees that reached over the water. But at this very moment, everything around me seemed bereft! There was no beauty. Life seemed utterly empty and meaningless. Nothing seemed real anymore. Mechanically, I positioned myself into one of the armchairs by the window. I was ready. No, I wasn't ready. Thinking about my son's young family was breaking my heart into millions of tiny pieces. My heart ached for Cheryl and for my four precious grandchildren. Oh God, my four young, fatherless grandchildren!

I steeled myself as I prepared to speak with my daughter-in-law. Finally I pushed the button on my cell phone favorites menu and held my breath as Cheryl's number dialed. When she answered, I knew immediately that angels were attending her as well. She didn't tell me about them. And I did not hear them. I just knew, because she was still Cheryl. My daughter-in-law was remarkably composed.

We talked only briefly. Then Cheryl quietly asked, "Did Ken tell you that Max is with him?"

My God! *No!* Not Max too! My bedroom was spinning. Not both my son and my grandson! Please, not Cheryl's child! I needed to wake up. This could only be a horrid nightmare. The rhythm of my heartbeat echoed in my ears. Time seemed to pass in slow motion. And there was more bad news! Max's good friend, Ryan, was also with them.

The sheriff was calling Cheryl. She would call me back when she knew more. So far, no one knew when or where they'd gone down. Oregon is covered in trees. There are mountains and hills and millions of trees covering the rugged Oregon landscape. When I was again on the phone with Kenny, my grieving firstborn son soberly confided, "I just couldn't tell you about Max and Ryan."

The rest of that fateful Tuesday was a blur. Only flashes of memory remain. I wanted to have faith that they were still with us. I tried to hold that faith, as if through sheer will I could bring about a change of fate. I asked for prayers from family and friends. We needed lots of prayers. Soon, we received phone calls and visits. Friends and my sister, Reni, sat with us through that long, difficult day. My two nieces drove down from Anthem. We all sat around and waited in quiet, sorrowful disbelief. I felt strangely disconnected yet perfectly aware that I wasn't thinking straight. I was numb. Sudden emotional shock protects the human body from extreme physical pain. That comes later—in full force. Listless, we sat around the kitchen table desperately hoping for some positive news. Eventually, we learned a backpack had washed ashore in Brookings. It was found by a couple strolling along the beach. The backpack was identi-

fied as belonging to Ryan. My sister had found an
online link to Channel 13 KVAL:

> GRANTS PASS, Ore.—The Coast
> Guard suspended its search
> for three people at 9:47 p.m.
> Tuesday after more than 12 hours
> of searching for survivors of a
> downed aircraft near Brookings.
>
> The U.S. Coast Guard
> took over the search after a back-
> pack and other items believed
> to belong to one of the people
> aboard the plane washed ashore
> near Lone Ranch Picnic Park,
> 4 miles north of the Brookings
> Airport on the Oregon Coast.
>
> "It appeared the items had
> floated ashore indicating that the
> plane must have crashed into the
> ocean," Sheriff John Ward said in
> a press release.

Bit by bit we learned of the events leading up to
the flight. After his shift in Salinas ended early morning on Monday, July 4, John flew into Brookings to
join his family. Cheryl picked him up at the local
airport. Along with their four children, she'd brought
Max's good friend Ryan.

John and Cheryl and the kids had spent the hol-
iday enjoying the beach and the ocean. They'd stayed

in Brookings through the evening to watch the display of fireworks on the harbor. At some point, Ryan, who had never flown in an airplane, was invited to fly home with John. Aware that Max wasn't comfortable flying in that small plane, I wondered if my grandson went along just to support his friend?

Little Ashlynn didn't like to fly either. One time, only, did John take his youngest daughter up in the airplane. This became an exceptionally short flight. Once in the air, John looked back at his little girl and recognized immediately that she was terrified. Ashlynn had nodded emphatically when John asked if she wanted him to take the plane down. Only Luke and Reagan were seasoned flyers. Like their father, they loved cruising high above the earth against the eternal heavenly sky.

Chapter 3

The world looks so strangely different when you suddenly experience severe loss. Everyone around you seems to be going about daily living as usual. All the while "normal" has so tragically disappeared from your sphere. It seems you are no longer part of everyday life. Rather, you're observing life from a whole different vantage point. You may wish to hit a delete button. But there isn't one. There is absolutely nothing you can do about it. Your fate is unalterable and so excruciatingly final. It utterly changes how you feel about yourself and about everything and everyone around you. Suddenly, you are no longer who you always were.

My husband and I landed in Medford early evening on Wednesday and drove directly to Grants Pass. Many times we'd driven this route in the past nine years—always eagerly anticipating the happy reunion with our loved ones. This evening there was a palpable emptiness surrounding us. It was as if the early evening sky along with the mountains and the tall trees bordering the freeway were aware and mourning with us, that John and Max and Ryan were gone forever from this life. It was so utterly heartbreaking to consider that husband, father, and teenage son would never again in this lifetime join Cheryl and their three remaining children in their home on the hill. They were so brave when they greeted us. That's what I remember. They were brave. Otherwise, my mind has erased the memory of our arrival to their home. What permeated my whole being was a deep, sorrowful feeling of emptiness and void. And pain within my soul like fire.

As usual, the next morning, the girls were up early. I left our bed and quietly closed the door to Max's bedroom, where Robin lay sleeping. Downstairs I fixed breakfast for my two granddaughters. Their happy chatter lifted my spirit. Reagan started singing. She is a beautiful and graceful ten-year-old girl with natural brunette curls cascading down her back. She enjoys playing with her little sister. Together they spend much time erecting buildings with their many Lego blocks. Dolls have never been her thing. Reagan likes having a friend over or going to a friend's house. She loves to dance, and she has been taking riding lessons. Both girls are learning to play the piano. I have enjoyed the opportunity to help Reagan with her homework. We FaceTime before school every morning. At seven, Ashlynn is a pretty little towhead. She's her mom's mini me. Quick and vivacious, she is always busy with something. Her dolls go everywhere with her. Rarely are her arms empty. If not carrying her dolls, she has the black family cat in her arms, or she's strolling the cat around in her doll stroller. This full-grown feline obliges her young mistress, even if swaddled in a blanket. Though, Ashlynn has several obvious scratches along both arms.

Both girls were singing. Song can be a form of prayer. They know this. But did they truly grasp that their beloved daddy and big brother Max were gone from our earthly lives for as long as we each live? Even I couldn't seem to grasp this new reality. Grandpa eventually joined us, and Reagan and Ashlynn jumped at the chance to go to the store with him. They would help him pick out donuts. He started a tradition of bringing back a dozen donuts during one of our many visits to Grants Pass. Sometime later, Luke and two friends lumbered into the kitchen. They'd been bedded down in the large media room over the garage. Cheryl's sister, Dianne, and two of Cheryl's close friends were also at the house. And Cheryl's mother arrived sometime before midnight.

Later that morning, I discovered that Luke had posted to Instagram:

> Oh Max you were the best brother a bro could have. You were there for me when I was bored or even sad. You made me laugh all the time in the best way. You were the best to the little sisters and you knew just what to do when they were sad. You were athletic kind and loving. I love you. [He had added two heart emoticons.]

Oh Ryan you were always at our house. You did everything with him and me. You were part of the family cause you made my sisters laugh all the time and me. You were adventurous and daring and that's why you're the best. Hopefully we can laugh about that weird rainstorm that went off and on later.

John Luke Belnap, you were the best out of them all. You always had something up your sleeve and knew just what to do in any case of scenario. I don't know how it happened, but however it happened you knew what to do. I'm going to miss you and I know hundreds of others will miss you all. You had the best life and I can't wait to see you again.

Luke closed his posting with two heart emoticons. My grandson is a tender soul. From now until the end of his days, Luke will be assuming the role of eldest child in this family.

Cheryl's sister, Dianne, and her friends were her warriors. They huddled with her in her bedroom, where they were planning and choosing family pictures to be included in a video Cheryl was preparing for the service. Though we still had no knowledge of the whereabouts of our loved ones, the service had been scheduled for Monday.

My daughter-in-law barely ate. Grief was edged onto her features. Her expression was beyond sadness and registered pain in my very bones. Our hearts were shattered. We wanted them back. The feeling of loss was overwhelmingly painful. Yet we all kept it together. What good will it do to fall apart? I had prayed so earnestly that my family would never again have to endure this kind of separation. After all, most pilots live long lives. But here we are now, living this new reality—a tragic repeat of the past! My beautiful grandchildren must grow up without their father's love and guidance. It seemed so utterly unjust. Even their big brother was gone. Boys and girls from Grants Pass High School stopped by. Openly they shed tears. Each shared memories of Max. He was their top track and cross-country runner. Took the lead right from the start of his freshman year. The sudden tragic deaths of their two friends would always be part of the memory of their high school years. They would never forget. Graciously, Cheryl allowed these young friends access to Max's room. She allowed them to choose a keepsake. Death is a great equalizer. Max will no longer need his things. He will not need his closet full of clothes. Nor will he need his treasured white jeep that sat ghostlike in the garage. One day while Max was outside working on his jeep, it had started to roll off the side of their hill. He'd thought of jumping in front of it to make it stop. "But I thought better of it, Grandma," he'd said to me. Fortunately, the damage was negligible. His car didn't get far. But were it not for the many trees on their property, his jeep would have ended up at the bottom of a forty-foot ravine.

Area news stations continued to provide regular updates.

> "… Curry County Sheriff's Search and Rescue members walked the coastline from Whales Head State Park to Harris Beach State Park looking for any items or indications of a plane crash. SAR members did find several other items that are believed to have been from the plane.
>
> Josephine County Sheriff Dave Daniel and his SAR Coordinator, Deputy Cory Krauss, responded to Curry County to provide assistance as John Belnap is a Josephine County SAR member, Sheriff Ward said.
>
> The Coast Guard currently has aircrews aboard a C-27J Spartan fixed-wing aircraft from Air Station Sacramento, California, and a Dolphin helicopter on scene and searching the area.

A boat crew from Station
Chetco River in Brookings is also
searching. (Channel 13 KVAL)"

Ryan's parents stopped by midafternoon.
Grieving deeply their loss of the youngest of their
three sons, this thoughtful, stoic couple came
to extend their condolences. Late that evening,
the bishop came to finalize discussion regarding
Monday's service. The Belnap home was filled to
the brim with family and friends. Even with a full
house, the feeling of raw emptiness was hauntingly
discernible. Countless prayers were offered on behalf
of our family. These many prayers held us up. As did
the caring efforts of untold individuals who were
engaged in finding the plane and bringing back our
loved ones. Thankfully, there are many wonderful,
selfless people in this world. People ready and willing
to give of their time and even risk their own lives on
behalf of strangers. John had derived deep satisfac-
tion from participating with those brave search and
rescue divers from Josephine County. For eight years
he'd trained and donated countless hours along with
all other members of Josephine County SAR team.
His buddies were looking for him now. Thankfully,
they were not willing to give up on one of their own.
Contacted by Newswatch 12, Cheryl released
the following statement:

The Belnap Family is deeply
grateful for the outpouring of

love and kindness that has been shown to our family. We would like to thank all those involved in the search for John, Max, and Ryan. We especially appreciate the US Coast Guard, Civil Air Patrol, Search and Rescue teams, and local Sheriff Departments in addition to the many private individuals who donated their time and airplanes to join in the search. We extend our deepest sympathy to the family and friends of Ryan Merker. We consider Ryan part of our family and will miss him. We feel strengthened by the thousands of individual prayers being said on our behalf.

Without an actual location for the crash site, the task of finding the plane proved monumental. Though several days had passed, only the plane's nosewheel had been found. It had lodged in the rocks off the Oregon coast. With each passing day we became painfully aware that the ocean might never release our loved ones from their watery grave.

Thursday evening I caught a portion of the daily news on TV just as a newscaster announced that a local woman had observed the lights of an airplane flying somewhat lower than was usual over her home on the night of July 4. She'd followed the plane's flight path over the ocean. Moments later she'd heard a crunching sound. *Was this the plane crashing?* That thought was quickly dismissed with thoughts of late fireworks. But when she watched the newscast about the missing plane the next morning, she'd become convinced that she had indeed witnessed the final moments of a pilot's flight.

A longtime scuba diver, Ken desperately wanted to assist in the search. I was grateful the local sheriff steadfastly refused to give his permission. As day after day passed with no positive news, my son defeatedly lamented, "John would not have left me out there!" Because our conversation led to the witness I had observed on the evening newscast, Ken quickly contacted the sheriff in Brookings. He was soon shown the exact flight path observed by the woman on that fateful July night. As search efforts again resumed, this time in the direction of the noted flight path, several oil spots were discovered on the ocean surface. A white garment had floated up from below. Kenny was able to identify this T-shirt as a garment belonging to his brother.

Thankfully, the divers now had a more probable location to concentrate their valiant efforts. These caring and dedicated individuals continued to work tirelessly. We felt enveloped by their love and concern. The cross-country coach from Grants Pass High School, Stan Godell, was such an individual. Godell stayed in Brookings for days. Stayed for his two boys. This incredible, selfless youth leader stayed on in the hope of being available to identify the bodies of Max and Ryan so we wouldn't have to.

Genevieve Reaume from Newswatch 12 reported from Brookings, Oregon:

> After four days of searching, rescue crews are unable to find the missing plane that crashed near Brookings on the Fourth of July. Inside the plane was John Belnap, his 17-year-old son, Max and Max's friend, Ryan Merker. Both boys were going into their senior year at Grants Pass High School. There were two sonar boats out on the water today, multiple divers went under, but the water was too rough to work in. But there's one man who's been there the whole time. He isn't on the search and rescue team or with any sheriff's offices. "Be strong, never quit, never give up." That's what Stan Goodell, Max and Ryan's cross country coach, has been doing every day. Holding back tears he says why. "It's my life, it's what I do," Goodell said. It's what he preaches up those hills, around those bends. In the final stretch. "The 100 meters,

Max just poured it on and he ran a sub 60, he ran 58 seconds," Goodell said. It's also what Max did in his final workout with the team Monday morning. "He said, 'Coach I feel really good,' and I said, 'You could have a great season if you want,' and he said, 'That's cool.' That's a lasting memory that I'm going to hold close and deep in my heart," Goodell said. "Max was ready to take the team to state. Ryan was ready to break top seven. Both were ready to take on senior year. They definitely stood out, everybody knew them," Goodall said. So for them, Goodell stays and searches, "I just have to be here," Goodell said.

My son Kenny, who rarely posted to Facebook, left following message for his friends:

I love you, Brother. John Belnap and his son Max were suddenly taken from us on Monday 7/4. Our hearts are broken. Please pray for his wife Cheryl, son Luke, and daughters Reagan and Ashlynn. We will see you both

again and until then, we will miss
you dearly with every day that
passes.

Sitting on the floor in Max's bedroom, I con-
templated my son's somber Facebook posting.
Already, four mornings had dawned since we awoke
to this devastating nightmare. Except this was no
nightmare. This was our new reality. Inexplicably,
the pain of this tragedy steadily weaved itself into the
fabric of our daily lives.

Staring up at Max's closet, where his clothes
still hung so neatly, I leaned up against the bed.
My grandson slept in this bed a few short days ago.
Before his mother's world fell apart. Before the secure
childhoods of his three younger siblings were forever
altered. Very recently Max had coined the phrase,
"Admire life while it lasts." *Had Max sensed a change
was coming?*

My thoughts lingered with Ryan's family. Like
ours, their grief was great—an empty void. "A hole
never again to be filled," said Darren Merker, Ryan's
father. Excited for their son to have the experience
of flying in an airplane, they'd given their permission. "We said, 'You bet, have fun, and we love you,'"
Ryan's grieving father was thus quoted by NBC News.
That was the last they heard of their youngest son.

All three were young and vital. John was needed
so very much here with us as husband, father, son,
brother, and friend. He was at such a great place in
his life. My grandson was a seventeen-year-old kid.

That ought to be too young to be allowed to die. His mother needed her firstborn son. His siblings needed their older brother. All three were needed here with us, their family! But it does no good to think like that. That's asking for more pain, and I already know better.

Many were praying and sending their love. And I had again felt the "balm of Gilead," that peace that surpasses all understanding. But until yesterday, I didn't pray. What good does it do? Hadn't I been praying for more than a year that my good son John would be the kind of pilot who lived a long life? Most pilots live a long life! But *God* didn't listen! *He* already had John's father and our two youngest children exactly the same way—a tragic plane crash! Doesn't *he* know that was already too much? So why talk to him. He's obviously going to have it his way. I wasn't angry. It was more a feeling of pained indifference. So I turned my back like a child not getting her way.

We were on an emotional roller coaster. And I despise roller coasters. Decided years ago I would never get on another one. Sweet granddaughter Jayme was eight the last time I went. She had so much fun, while I screamed—and not for joy. Jayme is twenty-five now. Fortunately, my faith is stronger than my roller-coaster emotions. And I know the day will come when I will get to see the bigger picture. I have felt Christ walking with me shoulder to shoulder, giving me of his strength. I have never seen his face. But there have been times when he's pulled me along like a screaming, kicking four-year-old, because I couldn't do it anymore. Christ told me I could. He lent me his strength, and then I could. He will do this for me again. Christ is there for our whole family. But it will forever be our individual choice to invite him in.

It gives me comfort to know this for my sweet daughter-in-law. Christ is there for Cheryl, who will need to raise her children without their father. She is strong. She's a good and loving mom. And she's also firm. My son John was a devoted husband. A loving father. John and Cheryl crammed so much living into their family life since they wed in December 1992. They worked hard to make it a good marriage. It wasn't always easy. But they persevered. They did everything together. Traveled, waterskied, snowskied, scuba-dived. The boys scuba-dived from age twelve. John's capacity for cramming twenty-nine hours into twenty-four was shared by his bishop. They were a wonderful family! And this is not the end—it is a new beginning. Cheryl and the children will find their way through Christ.

A soothing, comforting peace had thankfully enveloped me and once again eased the pain in my heart. Though I knew the next wave of grief will hit whenever I least expect it. It hits hard. How is it possible that my heart can be so utterly broken and yet feel such reassuring peace? A juxtaposition! "Be still and know that I am God" (Psalms 46:10).

Chapter 4

Pioneer stories fascinated me when I was a young girl. How did the pioneers find strength to continue on their way in spite of extreme personal losses? Faithful and stalwart they walked on, even when spouses, babies, or parents and siblings were lost to death along the way. They bravely walked on through debilitating, freezing cold, through soaking rain or scorching desert sun. They had faith in Christ. They relied on him. They knew where they were going. And they knew why. Fully and completely, their faith sustained them. Like the pioneers, I am determined to place my trust in my Savior. I know he can bring me through this monumental loss and deep sadness. Daily joy is possible, even when living with tragedy. Thankfully, I know this.

The deadline for the obituaries was approaching. We all worked on this together. There was such finality in and through these days. It was the end of our lives as we had known it. Friends dropped off favorite dishes and Relief Society sisters brought dinners for the many mouths to be fed in the Belnap home on the hill. Beautiful floral arrangements and large plants steadily arrived. The generosity extended to Cheryl and her children was an immense blessing. The love offered was palpable. It was reassuring to know that John's family had the support of so many wonderful friends. For it takes a long time to heal from loss. Some never do.

> JOHN LUKE BELNAP—John Luke Belnap was born to Karin and Roger Belnap on December 9, 1969, in Phoenix, Arizona. He and his son Max returned to their loving Heavenly Father on July 4, 2016, in a small plane crash along the Oregon coast near Brookings. John graduated from Arcadia High School in Phoenix, Arizona, class of 1988, and served a two-year mission in Denmark for the LDS church. He later graduated from Arizona State University and went on to get his master's degree from UNCG in Raleigh, North Carolina. John was a CRNA (Nurse Anesthetist) at Asante Three Rivers Medical Center, where he worked for more than eight years. John married his sweetheart, Cheryl Romney, for time and all eternity in the LDS Mesa Arizona Temple on December 19, 1992, and

together they have four beautiful children. John was a devoted member of the Church of Jesus Christ of Latter-Day Saints and held many positions of leadership. He was dedicated to the Boy Scout program and was known to plan amazing scout camps, outings, and fund-raisers. John was active in his community, and a member of the Josephine County Search and Rescue Dive Team. John had a drive for adventure and a passion for flying. He was a devoted husband and father and took every opportunity to spend time with his family. The family took frequent vacations and loved to enjoy these experiences of life together. John had a truly positive impact on people throughout areas of his life from work to family, church, and community. He will be sorely missed by all. John is survived by his wife, Cheryl; their children, Luke, Reagan, Ashlynn; mother, Karin, and stepfather, Robin; brothers, Mark, Ken, Aaron, and Alec; sister, Stacy; and countless aunts, uncles, nieces, nephews, and cousins. John is preceded in death by his father, Roger Belnap; brother, Jedd; and sister, Leslie. Services will be held on Monday, July 11 at 10:00 a.m. at the Church of Jesus Christ of Latter-Day Saints, 1969 Williams Hwy., Grants Pass, Oregon.

MAXEL JED BELNAP
"Admire life while it lasts."—Max

Maxel "Max" Jed Belnap was born to John and Cheryl Belnap on April 27, 1999, in Scottsdale, Arizona. He and his father, John, returned to their loving Heavenly Father on July 4, 2016, in a small plane crash along the Oregon coast near Brookings. Max was seventeen years old and a student at Grants Pass High School, and he lived life to the fullest. He loved life, adventure, his family and his friends. Max was a good student, a top athlete, an Eagle Scout, involved in leadership, orchestra, a member of the National Honors Society, and he volunteered in his free time. Max loved to be active and encouraged his peers to "go out and try new things." He was a loyal, kind, and loving friend. He loved his family and the adventures he had with them. He was devoted to his family, his LDS faith, and his gift for running. Max is survived by his mother, Cheryl; brother, Luke; sisters, Reagan and Ashlynn; loving grandparents; and countless aunts, uncles, and cousins. Max left us way too early and will be dearly missed. His legacy of grace and dignity will live on through the lives he touched. Max admired life and we will always admire Max. Services will be held on Monday, July 11 at 10:00 a.m. at the Church of Jesus Christ of Latter-Day Saints, 1969 Williams Hwy., Grants Pass, Oregon.

Later that afternoon, a memory surfaced from a few years ago, when John took his wife to Denmark, where he'd served a two-year mission for our church. Their trip included London and Paris. Finally, they had arrived back in Phoenix, and I received a text they'd be with us shortly. Though it was a blazing-hot afternoon in July, my granddaughters and I went outside to await their arrival. The two little girls were beyond excited to see their parents again.

At last, they pulled onto our driveway. John quickly got out. His arms opened wide. Pure joy radiated from the flushed, excited faces of his precious little girls as they practically flew into the loving arms of their daddy. I will forever cherish this memory—a sweet, loving moment tucked deep into my heart. And I know Reagan and Ashlynn will again experience this feeling of pure joy when they are finally reunited and again enveloped in their daddy's loving embrace.

Still no sign of the plane wreckage, and by Sunday bad weather hampered the search. With only three to five feet visibility, all efforts were temporarily halted. On standby for better weather, these good men were not willing to give up.

"We're still hitting it," said Josephine County Sheriff Dave Daniel. "We're not going to quit, at least not for now."

Years back when John shared with me that he had joined the local search and rescue team, he'd just finished training in the Rogue River. His team had been diving all that day in murky water. Could see only a foot ahead. My silent wish that day had been that my son could have chosen a less dangerous way to give service.

Grief counseling was made available at Grants Pass High School, where a vigil was held the day after our loved ones went missing. Ryan's father had shared tender words with the assembled students.

"I want everyone to know, life is short. Give your mother and father a hug when you leave the house. You never know if it's the last time you're going to see them."

On the mountain behind the high school was painted a large white "MRJ." All of Grants Pass was mourning Max, Ryan, and John. Our last time spent with Max was at his Eagle Court of Honor, when he was still sixteen. He'd spoken humbly and eloquently to family, friends, and leaders who gathered to honor him. His goal was to study to become an ophthalmologist. Already, his plan was firmly laid out. Strong, handsome, and popular, he was an exceptional youth with many talents. And he was humble and kind. Time is so fleeting. In the twinkling of an eye, it can all be snatched away.

At eight, I started to take an interest in news stories on the radio and in our daily paper. I hungered for facts and details. But this week it has once again become personal. Repeatedly, their names are mentioned. Repeatedly, I hear that ominous word— tragedy. They left us much too soon and so suddenly! Only scattered memories of our loved ones and photos of our lives together are left behind. Photos that belong to another day and another time. But throughout this past week, relentlessly, photos of John and Max and Ryan are prominently displayed on the front page of *Grants Pass Daily Courier*. They're smiling in these front page photos, while journalistic words, in large bolded print, further assault our battered senses: TRIPLE TRAGEDY.

You cannot hide from grief. Loss intrudes, like a shadow, into every thought and every deed. It is not constant but often unrelenting in fierceness. And this pain of grief revisits again and again. Suddenly it consumes you. Like an ocean wave, it tosses and tumbles you about. You don't get to decide when pain lets go. There is no way around grieving. There is only through. You must walk through this invisible veil of sorrow. Friends and family can help. But mostly, it is a solitary walk. It changes you from the inside out. Grieving will take time. As you struggle with sadness, perhaps also with anger, despair, or regret, you may come to believe that living is not worth it. With time, you come to realize that you have choices. You can choose to look to God with faith and with hope in his eternal purposes. You can choose to accept what seems so utterly unacceptable. Faith and hope can propel you toward the happiness that has been promised in scriptures. In 2 Nephi, we read these hopeful words: "Man is that he might have joy." The healing power available through our Savior's atonement is real. A broken heart can be healed. A broken heart can find peace and joy through faith in Christ, who already suffered all things that we experience.

In Proverbs 3:5–6 we read, "Trust in the Lord with all thine heart; and lean not unto thine own understanding. In all thy ways acknowledge him, and he shall direct thy paths." It takes time to learn that happiness is not dependent upon circumstance. I didn't always know this.

While family and friends prepared to attend the Monday morning service on July 11, the search and rescue divers in Brookings took advantage of a small window of favorable weather to search the ocean for the missing plane.

It was a stunningly beautiful day as Robin and I arrived at the church. I marveled that all colors appeared vivid and intensified. The sky, a startling blue, was in deep contrast to the gray heaviness weighing upon my soul, and the familiar surroundings felt strangely foreign to me. Television cameras were set up on the freshly manicured green lawns in front of the meeting house. Reporters were on hand to record anyone willing to make a statement. No recording was allowed inside the chapel. Both the chapel and the adjoining cultural hall were soon filled to capacity. Additional seating was provided in several of the classrooms, where the service would be electronically transmitted. We found ourselves seated in front of two large portraits of John and Max, each flanking an elaborate floral arrangement. Robin was seated to my left. On my right was my granddaughter Reagan. On her right was Ashlynn, who was next to her mother. Luke was on Cheryl's right. Also with us was my impossible wish that this could be just a painful dream.

While we waited for the service to begin, a long-ago memory surfaced of a young John playing with his little sister and brother. On the stage of my mind, they were once again frolicking on the sandy beach at Crescent Bay. We'd spent countless warm and sunny days playing on that beach during family vacations. At that very moment I could see clearly into the distant past, now a lifetime away. Once again I watched my three youngest children at play—my beautiful sun-tanned kids laughing, running, and dancing so joyfully in the sand and surf on the sun-drenched coast of Southern California.

Crescent Bay was only a short walk from Grandma Belnap's house on PCH in Laguna Beach. Once upon a time, we could see the beach from her front porch. But that was long before homes crowded in on empty lots. My children's grandparents, aunts, uncles, and cousins lived in this idyllic coastal town, while John and his siblings were growing up.

Max was first to be eulogized, and Luke steadfastly stepped up to the podium. At the tender age of fourteen, my grandson is tall and slender. He read his older brother's obituary to the assembled crowd of more than one thousand in a clear and audible voice. Quietly composed, Luke then stepped away from the podium to sit again by his mother's side. I was comforted by the talks that followed. Both John and Max were accomplished, exemplary men. And they were kind. They were good. My heart was soothed. I hoped they got to listen in on this service to celebrate their lives.

An intermission showed a lovely video of family memories above the podium. A young friend to my grandson was at the piano playing Max's favorite piano piece, "Cannon in D." The exuberant love of life enjoyed by John and Cheryl's family was so plainly evident in this video. My soul wished for some magic way to shield my granddaughters from our tragic loss. I wanted pain gone from Luke and Cheryl. I know of the difficult road that lies ahead for them. Someone suggested to Luke that he was now man of the house. I assured him his mother was in charge and perfectly capable. But lending an extra hand could be a way for him to contribute. Luke earnestly offered, "That is exactly what I plan to do, Grandma." We are all proud of the strength this young man so courageously portrays in the face of this harsh adversity. He'd softly added, "They're the lucky ones, aren't they, Grandma?" It can sure seem like that to those of us left behind. Ashlynn didn't get to say goodbye. My petite seven-year-old grand-daughter fell asleep before her father and the two boys were dropped off at the airport in Brookings. Two hours passed quickly.

I will forever treasure the beautiful words spoken on behalf of my son and my grandson. I was grateful for their stellar examples. Both John and Max were accomplished, exemplary men. They were good and they were kind. For those of us left behind, there was comfort and a measure of healing in the loving words spoken during the memorial service. President Nelson, a surgeon, had praised John's work ethic. John was well respected by all who worked with him, was always calm and professional. He was a peacemaker.

"I was always happy to work with John," said the surgeon. I knew my patients would receive the best care, and I did not worry about them."

Does God speak to us parting words as we prepare to leave our heavenly home? Did He perhaps say to Max, "Go quickly, my son, and enjoy your turn on earth, for I'll need you back very soon!" Seventeen short years was all my grandson had. Yet Max lived his short life to the fullest. Always striving to do his best, he planned ahead and chose wisely. Not only was he handsome, smart, and good, Max was kind. And he was humble in his success. He had so recently coined the phrase "Admire life while it lasts." Had Max sensed, deep down in his youthful, intrepid soul, that he would not have many years? At nine, I was thrilled to be old enough to borrow books from the central library. With a shopping net full of books dangling from my handle bars, I pedaled my bike fast all that way home. These books filled me with excitement. It was more fun to read than to play. A special story has stayed with me for these many years. As has the line drawing depicting a cavernous room filled with candles that accompanied the story. There were candles that were exceptionally tall. Others were medium-sized. Some tall and fat or short and thin. Many were just a puddle of waxy substance! All depicted the lifespan of individuals, as measured by the various sizes of candles. This was the first time in my young life when I understood that we are each given an unknown number of days to live our lives. And that the length of our time on earth remains a mystery. God keeps this secret to himself! I always prayed for my loved ones to have extra thick and long candles. Fortunately, I did not know it then that God had other plans for my future. It surely seems the candles for both John and Max were years and years too short. Only God knows and understands the purpose and true reason for the shortened life span of our loved ones. It is our choice how we accept that loss, how we choose to go forward.

Chapter 5

The long line in the foyer was getting longer. Guests steadily filed by Cheryl to offer their condolences. My daughter-in-law stood resolute. One could plainly discern her heavy heart. Nothing could change the fact that her life had crumbled around her. Yet she was strong and brave. She would need to find a whole new path for herself, for her remaining young children. I pray for my daughter-in-law to be strong enough to continue to accept this harsh new reality. *Didn't I pray enough?* It's useless to go to this sorry place of self-pity. I know better. And something interesting happens if I start to seriously ponder, *Why my family?* Like a little white cloud in the sky, the questions simply blow away, and my heart feels only peace. That's when I know that I am loved and looked after from above, when my heart fills with that blessed peace that surpasses all understanding. A tender mercy! Thankfully, there are many tender mercies in my life. God is omnipotent. He has unlimited power. Deep in my heart I believe this. With unlimited power, he could have prevented this tragic accident. And from the bottom of my heart, I wish God would have done just that. But that is not what happened. For the time being, God asks that I put my trust in him and in his son, my elder brother. Through the grace of the atonement of Jesus Christ, I am able to do that.

God is also omniscient. He is all-knowing, all-wise, and all-seeing. His timetable differs from ours. Life is often just plain hard. Life wasn't easy for our savior. Our elder brother, Jesus Christ, was born to suffer infinitely more than any of us will ever be asked to suffer. He was the perfect son! The only perfect being to walk this earth. Yet he endured unimaginable suffering. How difficult it must have been for God to withhold his powers. He could have stopped it. Even Christ had this power to stop his own suffering. Yet he endured for our sake. Years ago, a visitor to our ward shared his testimony with our congregation. Along with several members of his family, he was traveling on an icy highway when their van skidded onto the shoulder and rolled several times. No one was severely injured. Gratitude was expressed for this blessing. God was watching over them, he said. *Was God not watching over the boys and my son on that dark July night when John flew his plane into the ocean?* A challenging question. Fortunately, an answer has come to me. An answer I can accept. My blessing is that peace that surpasses all understanding. This remarkable peace has filled my soul again and again. *Be still and know that I am God.*

Following the service, a beautiful spread was provided for our large group by Relief Society sisters. Once again, there was the opportunity to visit and connect with family and friends. Many had traveled long distances to be with us. I felt robot-like as I smiled and laughed. That strange juxtaposition of laughter amid pain and tears!

Robin and I had made several trips to the Oregon coast along with John's family. Just last summer I'd waded into cold water to join the girls playing in a narrow lagoon. Both Reagan and Ashlynn seemed oblivious to the frigid temperature. The boys and John were body surfing. I didn't stay long in the cold water. Clearly, John's family had become true Oregonians. On that long-ago Saturday afternoon in Brookings, the sun had played hide-and-seek behind white cumulous clouds that floated quickly across a deep blue sky. It was a happy late summer beach excursion. We'd stopped for an evening meal at a local restaurant. Then enjoyed oversized ice cream cones from another place. Carefree, we'd lingered on sun-bleached benches while screeching seagulls landed all around us. Clearly used to scavenging for scraps among the tables, these large birds of the sea were not the least bit timid. Everything was so different now! This heavy feeling of loss and no getting away from intermittent onslaught of emotional pain. Yet we smile and laugh.

Family members were invited to gather at President Nelson's home for an evening buffet. On one side of their expansive green lawn was a large garden plot. On the other side, a playground for younger children. There was a trampoline. For several bizarre moments, my mind blocked completely why we were assembled in that backyard. On the trampoline before me, I watched Max jump and do flips with two other boys. Then the realization hit me, that my grandson could not be the one jumping on that trampoline. Ashlynn and Reagan came racing across the lawn. They were headed to the far end of the property, to a thicket with wild blackberry bushes. Their cousins and friends were right behind them. All had large red plastic cups for gathering berries. *Were the girls as lighthearted as they seemed? They were so young. How could they possibly understand the long-reaching effects of the past week?*

Our group lingered. We stayed longer than I thought we would, or probably should. It was time to give that lovely home back to our host family. All had been so gracious. That evening I received a short video from Cheryl. It was of John blowing a silent kiss. His final goodnight kiss, all but two seconds long. She played it before bed with her children. Obsessively I watched it over and over. It is seared into my brain.

That same day, in Brookings, John's dive team from Josephine County had three members searching the ocean where the plane went down. The continued efforts and dedication by John's teammates touched me deeply. I had worried when John occasionally shared stories of his training exercises. Over the past week I gained appreciation and a new perspective. It had meant the world to him to be part of this brotherhood, to be of service. How grateful we felt for the dedicated efforts of so many thoughtful and concerned individuals so willing to give of their time!

Reagan and Ashlynn did not forget that Grandma had promised lunch and a shopping trip. My sister joined us. Reni had been with me for most of this difficult week. Time crept up on us. It was well past noon before we finally headed to the park with our picnic lunch from KFC.

A flock of Canadian geese waddled up from the picturesque Rogue River floating lazily below. Apparently, it was lunchtime for them too, and they seemed to have a plan. They headed straight for us and consumed most of our lunch. Somehow, none of us were very hungry. A large goose suddenly went after Ashlynn. Unperturbed, she chased that big brown bird away. My petite seven-year-old blond granddaughter is fearless. Baskin Robbins was next on our agenda. The girls ordered chocolate-covered waffle cones with sprinkles. Anything they wanted. As if that could make up for all that was lost. I functioned automatically. My heart was weeping. Yet my eyes stayed dry. Perhaps, we are all just actors on this stage called life. Later that evening, I succeeded in coaxing Luke and his two friends out of the media room for another trip to Baskin Robbins. More huge helpings of ice cream and several extra cartons for the freezer! The exact location of the plane crash had stayed hidden for eleven long days. High winds and rough seas continued to hamper the search. With swells as high as eight or more feet, it was far too risky for the divers to go down. The weather outlook for the remainder of the week was no better. Sheriff Ward promised the search would continue "until we run out of resources." I try not to think about our loved ones lying somewhere on that vast ocean floor. They live in another sphere. I picture them happy and involved. They are settling in and learning the ropes of their new existence. Seems strange, when thinking like this, I can almost be happy for them. They have gone home. Our earthly abode is not our real home.

Alaska Air took us back to Arizona. I miss the way it used to be. Robin and I resumed walking early mornings. But I also walk alone. I walk for miles, to push through the pain. I already know that my attitude can make me or break me. It does no good to allow negative thoughts to occupy my mind. With time, I have come to understand the importance of choosing carefully my thoughts. Maudlin thoughts can only take me to a place where I don't want to be. It is entirely my choice which thoughts I allow to take center stage in my mind. Rather than ruminate over things in my life that cannot be changed, I can focus on my blessings. I can replace negative thoughts with thoughts of gratitude.

"Continue steadfastly in prayer, being watchful in it with thanksgiving" (Colossians 4:2).

There is power in the scriptures. And joy. It is astonishing to me that I can walk through this dark valley of grief and still find joy in living. Our elder brother, Jesus Christ, knows and understands personally what we face during our earthly journey. He can make our burdens light. But he will never force himself upon us. We must first open the door to our hearts and let him in. As we reach out through daily prayer and scripture study, he will minister to us through the Holy Ghost.

In 1995, President Gordon B. Hinckley said, "I am grateful for the emphasis on reading the scriptures. I hope that for you this will become something far more enjoyable than a duty; rather it will become a love affair with the word of God. I promise you that as you read, your minds will be enlightened and your spirits will be lifted. At first it may seem tedious, but that will change into a wondrous experience with thoughts and words of things divine."

In the words of President Russell M. Nelson, "When I think of the Book of Mormon, I think of the word power. The truths of the Book of Mormon have the power to heal, comfort, restore, succor, strengthen, console, and cheer our souls." As I read his words, I am reminded of the Old Testament story in Numbers 21. The bites of poisonous serpents caused many of the Israelites to die. They asked Moses to petition the Lord to have the serpents taken away. The Lord responded with a lesson on faith: "And the Lord said unto Moses, Make thee a fiery serpent, and set it upon a pole: and it shall come to pass, that every one that is bitten, when he looketh upon it, shall live. And Moses made a serpent of brass, and put it upon a pole, and it came to pass, that if a serpent had bitten any man, when he beheld the serpent of brass, he lived" (Numbers 21:8–9).

Most could not be bothered. Was it too easy?

Max was first to be brought up. The long, agonizing wait was finally over. More than two weeks had passed since the search began. It had seemed like searching for a needle in a hay stack. The next day, the SAR team found John. More easily identified by his wedding band, he was found a short distance away from the plane. The dedicated diving teams continued their search for Ryan, until Oregon's ever-changing coastal weather once again rendered it unsafe for the divers to go down. Because of rough seas, it was unclear when the search would resume. Not so long ago John had reminded me of the need to write down every specific desire we might wish to have carried out after our passing. That day, on the phone, he and I had joked about the subject at hand. The two of us could become quite irreverent when discussing topics of human demise.

Chapter 6

My daughter-in-law and grandkids stayed at our house on their long drive south to visit her family. Cheryl and her siblings were raised in Colonia Juarez, in the state of Chihuahua in Mexico. This area is commonly referred to as the Mormon Colonies. Her parents still live there, as do her two brothers with their families. In August they returned to us. I took my grandkids to Del Taco that night—their dinner choice, not mine. They'd feasted on enchiladas and quesadillas every single day while in Mexico but apparently had not yet had enough. Cheryl had invited a friend of Luke's along to keep him company. As we chatted, I learned that this young man had several older brothers.

"We have only one brother now," Ashlynn quietly interjected.

Her little face exuded sadness and resignation. In my feeble attempt to reassure her, I explained, "Sweetheart, you will always have two brothers. It's just… Daddy and Max live somewhere else now."

Sometime before noon on Sunday, August 7, Ryan's body was recovered farthest removed from the plane. Five divers were part of the search efforts that morning. The long wait had been difficult for all involved. The steadfast search by the SAR teams will forever be imprinted on our hearts. These men are true heroes. Very often the burdens encountered in this life can seem too heavy to carry. In various forms they come to most of us. Some become angry at the fate handed them. Perhaps I am just too tired for such an overwhelming emotion. It takes much negative energy to be angry. I had prayed so earnestly that John be protected, that my son be the kind of pilot whose life is long. I can only guess that God had reasons for wanting it his way the night of that fatal flight.

There's really only one way to survive this difficult loss. And that is to surrender, completely, to God's will.

Chapter 7

In October, I was back in Oregon taking care of my grandkids while Cheryl spent a week with her family. Several changes had been made to the Belnap home. They were building a new life for themselves. Each of the children occupied a different bedroom. Reagan had begged her mom to be in Max's room. I admired Cheryl that she did not turn her firstborn child's room into a shrine. Each day was a flurry of activities, and the week flew by in a flash. Reagan had a riding lesson. A graceful child, she sat perfectly straight in her saddle while her horse trotted around the arena. She was excited for her birthday to arrive, and presents were already lined up by the fireplace. I suggested we celebrate by going to her favorite restaurant, an Asian place in Medford. We'd all been there before with John and Max. Three kids filled up on noodles then begged to go to the nearby Rogue Air Trampoline Park. I protested; their stomachs were full. They assured me that wouldn't matter. So I watched as they literally bounced off the walls around this indoor park. And I was the only dizzy one. I was scheduled to fly into Phoenix shortly before midnight. Though Robin's night vision has deteriorated, he insisted on picking me up at the airport. He brought along his briefcase with work to do and drove to the airport while it was still light out. I could easily have taken a taxi home. But he wanted to be there for me. I am deeply grateful for my caring husband's steady, loving support. He is one of my tender mercies. On November 4, Luke posted a photo to Instagram—the photo shows him with his dad and older brother where train tracks crossed a bridge. Happy smiles lighted youthful, boyish faces. They were always a tight threesome. Luke's caption read, "It's been 4 long months since I've seen them. Hasn't been easy, but I like to live by this quote, 'When life gives you 100 reasons to frown, give it 1,000 reasons to smile!'"

The very absence of our loved ones is a presence all its own, and a palpable emptiness was felt around our Thanksgiving table. But it was a good week celebrated with family. We lodged at Stacy's beach house. While new memories were made in this old familiar place, I entertained my grandchildren with family lore. Their father had spent many memorable days at this very beach house during his childhood. As did their grandfather, Roger, an avid surfer. Roger had lived in this home through most of his teen years. The home was originally purchased by Grandpa and Grandma Belnap in the late 1940s. They'd moved from Riverside, California, after their two eldest children left home to attend BYU. In January of 1999, after Grandma Belnap also passed away, Stacy persuaded her younger brothers, Ken and John, to purchase the old family home with her. Their inheritance from the estate was pooled as down payment. This place is her baby—she has built it into a fine vacation rental business.

Chapter 8

A new normal prevails as the days of our lives continue. Firsts are difficult, pain still fresh and raw. My son's forty-seventh birthday came only five months and five days after they left us. John was my Christmas baby. He entered our world precisely at 9:32 a.m. on Tuesday, December 9, 1969. Though John was delivered with forceps, it was an easy birth. From beginning to end, I labored for only two hours. And I was immediately starving. The day my son would have celebrated his forty-seventh birthday, I awoke with pure joy in my heart. This sweet feeling of joy lasted throughout that whole day. It came from outside of me. It was surely a gift from above. A tender mercy! Ashlynn's birthday came just three days after her father's. She was now old enough to be baptized and as excited as any eight-year-old on her special day. Her baptism was scheduled for the last day of 2016. Our family would celebrate Ashlynn's baptism and start the new year by spreading the ashes of our loved ones along the rugged coast of Oregon. With so many family members already in town for Ashlynn's baptism, this seemed an appropriate time to bring closure to a very difficult chapter in our lives.

Chapter 9

It was Chloe's first Christmas, and the elusive Christmas spirit finally entered our hearts and our home with the arrival of Ken's family on Christmas Eve. Early morning, December 28, we set out for our two-day trek to Oregon. This time we had a deadline, and the weather was uncertain. There was the real possibility of snow over Siskiyou Pass. Cheryl had scheduled family dinner at one of their favorite restaurants, where we were to meet up with her extended family. A missed turn caused quite a delay. Free hot chocolate is served on Main Street in Grants Pass during Christmas season, and traffic proved unusually heavy that late Friday afternoon in this otherwise placid Oregon town. We were forced to detour by the hospital where John used to work. My heart was heavy here in their town.

Sunday's weather forecast was changing. All of Oregon was expecting heavy snow. It made sense to redo our carefully planned schedule. Thus, Saturday morning, as a pale winter sun peeked through scattered clouds, our group set out in four cars for the two-hour drive to the coast in Brookings. There was no immediate indication that stormy weather was approaching. Stacy had flown in from LAX early that morning. Mark drove up from southern California through the night. It was a beautiful day in Brookings. Intense sunshine blazed from a clear and cloudless blue sky. But most of us had bundled up for the low fifty-degree temperature. Ashlynn proved to be a real Viking. She made her way to the beach in a swimsuit. And stayed that way for the many hours we spent on the beach. The way to the cove leading from the highway to the beach below proved still muddy and slippery from recent rain. Several in our party needed a hand to make it all the way down this rugged, steep, and narrow path. From this location, one looked straight out to an enormous dark rock rising out of the frigid ocean water. To the right of this rock was the very spot where John's garment, or white T-shirt, had surfaced among oil formations. The tide was out that afternoon, and shallow tide pools were all around us. For most of July, the ocean had been rough. Often too rough for the divers to safely continue their search. On this sunny winter day, the ocean was like one gigantic, glassy, undulating and shimmering body of water. It was very dark that night when three mothers lost their sons. Why had John not recognized the absence of moonlight in the darkened sky? Or did he notice too late? Was he was getting ready to take the plane back to Brookings airport? What were his thoughts before he felt himself permanently propelled to that other side? Unanswered questions hang in the air. I wish I could ask him these questions. Inexplicably, after these many months, I can still forget that John can no longer share his experiences with me.

The day before the accident, while rummaging through a box of old stuff, I had come across an article in the Church News from 1975 which highlighted my parents. I had emailed the article to John and he had posed several questions concerning his Danish grandparents. This was John's final communication to me. Max and Ryan were texting with friends. Eventually, they no longer responded. I know John didn't want what happened. No pilot does. My son loved life. He had plans for the future. He loved flying. He loved his family deeply. And loved to work and interact with young men. John loved to teach them. He loved to show them a good time. It was Ryan's first flight. Did Max choose to come along only to share in Ryan's excitement? At seventeen, most youth feel they are invincible. Months before, Max had coined the phrase, "Admire life while it lasts." They were gone hours before anyone knew it. And there was absolutely no indication of what was in store as I awoke to that fateful July morning. It seems unfathomable now that I slept soundly through that dividing night that forever split our lives into before and after. Does one instantly gain a clearer perspective of mortality when emerging on the other side of that thin veil which here on earth clouds our memory of the preexistence? We know so little of God's eternal plan. But we know we were born to die. This world is not our real or final home. I wish John could call and tell me about his new experiences. And knowing this son of mine, I'm quite sure he wishes he could share with us what he has learned.

Our men built a fire. Large logs scattered along the beach were brought close and arranged in a circle for seating. This would be our last goodbye. Ken stayed in command of his emotions, spoke eloquently to our intimate group huddled around the now blazing fire. Mark opened the meeting with a tender prayer. Cheryl had painstakingly put together keepsakes for each of us. On the back of a card were photos of John and Max with dates of their life span. The front of the card depicted angels administering to a young woman. Attached was a small silver token depicting an angel. The word *brave* was engraved on a silver bar. "Be brave" was the Belnap family motto. John and Cheryl could hardly have imagined, when they chose brave to be their motto, just how very brave their family would need to be.

The small silver angel was a replica of a gift John had given to Cheryl. He'd quietly offered, "I thought you would like this." John was not generally sentimental. For that reason, his thoughtful gift was even more special to her. Grief, was etched into Cheryl's features as she spoke to us. Her heart was broken. Life would never be the same for her and for her children. But she had courageously carried the burden that was placed squarely upon her shoulders. John and Max are missed every single day. They live forever in our hearts. The spirit was strong that afternoon, as we shared thoughts and feelings around the fire. Ken offered a dedicatory prayer. How must it feel to offer a dedicatory prayer for a younger brother gone too soon? Even also for a teenage nephew? John was the sibling Ken had spent his childhood years with. My two boys had shared a room, not always peacefully, until Kenny was in his tenth year. There was a strong bond, a bond that will continue through the eternities. They will always be brothers, only John has now sprinted ahead. When they were little boys growing up, Kenny would occasionally loudly object to John copying him. I had to explain that his little brother was learning from him. And he, as the older brother, had the privilege of teaching. John has gone ahead, and perhaps he will be the teacher when they meet once again.

This cove on the rugged coast of Oregon will forever be a memorial to our loved ones. Already familiar with this area, Cheryl envisioned a memorial plaque fastened onto a towering dark rock that seemed to have emerged from the zillions of dry particles of sand covering the shore. Luke was selected for this task. Eventually, Reagan followed her brother to the top, where Luke sat with his head thoughtfully bowed. He is strong and resolute. My grandson's shoulders are broad and square. Luke will prevail. Our shadows grew long. The sinking sun was quickly making her way toward the horizon. Long-stemmed roses in hand, we walked out among the shallow tide pools. Soon, twenty-four red roses stood at rapt attention with loving words attached on small white notes. Gently, we spilled gray ashes from metal containers. In hallowed silence, we watched as ashes of our departed loved ones slowly widened their spread within the sandy tide pools. Very soon the mighty sea will flow back. Once again, it will take our loved ones to the depths that claimed their time with us. A haunting picture has imprinted itself in my mind. This raw image of my daughter-in-law and my three grandchildren standing at water's edge. They're facing the site, hundreds of feet from shore, where John's plane went down, where each of their lives, as they had known it, abruptly ended on that fateful July 4 night. They are waving into the brilliantly setting sun. Left behind, they wave their last farewell!

Chapter 10

The new year greeted us with a solid blanket of white. A slate-gray sky hung low over Grants Pass. Soon, it was snowing again. Weather reports for the weekend had correctly predicted a heavy winter storm for the state of Oregon. There were warnings of road closures.

"It's the climate." This catchy slogan is prominently displayed on a large banner hanging over 6th Street in city center. The generally moderate temperatures in this region is a source of local pride. Rarely had we seen snow on previous winter visits. But schools close their doors even when light snow flurries fall for the sake of children living in the surrounding mountains. The private driveway leading to the Belnap home is long and steep. As is the road that leads down to Williams Highway.

Snow was still falling when we arrived for Ashlynn's baptism. There was the feeling of reverence when looking through winter barren trees, as large feathery snowflakes floated ever so leisurely from above and silently blanketed the ground.

Customarily, baptisms take place in the ward building, where a baptismal font is available. But on Sundays, members assemble throughout the day for regularly scheduled meetings. Ashlynn's baptism was therefore to take place in a heated Jacuzzi at the home of Cheryl's friends. I fought back insistent tears and impossible thoughts of what should have been. It does no good to hold on to shoulds. Life is what it is. Ashlynn had chosen her Uncle Randy to baptize her. He was a longtime friend to John. His wife, Dianne, is the sibling closest to Cheryl. The two families shared many wonderful times in the past. Large snowflakes formed a crown covering Ashlynn's blond head, as her uncle gently took her hand and guided her into the warm water of the Jacuzzi. Baptism in our church is by full immersion, followed by the laying on of hands for the gift of the Holy Ghost. Grandpa Robin offered this blessing. Then Aunt Stacy gave a short talk about the gift of the Holy Ghost, a special gift that is bestowed upon every newly baptized member. In John 14:26 we read, "But the comforter, which is the Holy Ghost, whom the Father will send in my name, he shall teach you all things, and bring all things to your remembrance, whatsoever I have said unto you."

The words of Parley P. Pratt, an early church leader, resonate with me: "The Holy Ghost…quickens all the intellectual faculties, increases, enlarges, expands and purifies all the natural passions and affections and adapts them by the gift of wisdom, to their lawful use. It inspires virtue, kindness, goodness, tenderness, gentleness and charity. It develops beauty of person, form and features. It tends to give health, vigor, animation, and social feeling. It invigorates all the faculties of the physical and intellectual man. In short, it is, as it were, marrow to the bone, joy to the heart, light to the eyes, music to the ears, and life to the whole being…"

There were a lot of mouths to feed once everyone arrived back at the Belnap home following Sunday's regular church service. Robin and I broke our resolve to keep the Sabbath day holy. We stopped by the local Safeway to pick up a few items that were needed. By the checkout counter, the Sunday paper caught the corner of my eye. Bewildered, I turned to have a better look. I saw correctly! Three familiar faces once again smiled at me from the front page of the *Daily Courier*. The headline large and bold! Tears pooled in my eyes as I struggled to read, "The gripping search for the wreckage of a plane from Grants Pass that crashed almost without a trace off the Oregon coast was the top local story of 2016…" (Chris Bristol).

Chapter 11

At twenty-one, John returned from his two-year mission to Denmark with carpe diem in every fiber of his being. The day following his return, he'd eagerly shared details about an inspiring talk he'd heard. A fire was clearly burning in his soul. For him, there seemed to be no time to waste. John was determined to make the most of his life. Early in their marriage, John had shared with me a fear he harbored. He'd stopped by our house on the day he and Cheryl were getting ready to leave for a weeklong vacation. They'd be flying out of Phoenix Sky Harbor late that afternoon. His sun-blond hair was longer than usual, long enough to naturally curl. John was young, so ruggedly handsome, and bursting with youthful energy. Downstairs, in the kitchen, he'd turned to me and soberly confided, "Whenever I get on an airplane, I have the feeling that this will be the end." John was staring past me. "I can't shake it, Mom." In my attempt to lighten the tone, I'd responded feebly, "John, most planes don't crash." Had John experienced a premonition in his early youth? As a young boy, John was a white knuckle flyer. Even in childhood, he'd considered this weakness—not manly enough! Was his passion to fly to overcome his childhood fear? In due time, John experienced the ultimate of freedoms—the exhilaration of piloting his own airplane. Above our wildly beautiful and challenging world, John soared high against the endless deep blue sky. My son had indeed captured a true passion for flying. His jubilant smile told me this was so. John had overcome.

Untimely death of loved ones is a life-changing experience, emotionally devastating for family members left behind. Yet life must go on. Our time has not yet come. The very beginning of my own life story sprouted its roots during WWII, the day my father pointed to a map of Germany and randomly placed his finger on the city of Lobau.

Once upon a time many years ago, the old country road made a slight curve where it passed by the dairy plant. Directly across the street was a spacious green meadow. Except for a small opening, along that curving country road, the meadow was almost completely surrounded by the tall trees of a forest. For most of 1943, the young couple had lived in a tidy three-room abode above this newly constructed dairy plant in Varnsdorf, Czechoslovakia. Their small town was bordered by what would eventually become East Germany. In spite of WWII raging all around them, it was still fairly easy to cross the border. One only needed to bribe the guards. Friends and family from Germany visited quite often. In that humble home, on a cold and bleak winter's day, Traudel labored to give birth to their first child. When early morning dawned Monday, February 7, 1944, she'd already labored for more than twenty-four hours. Her strength almost gone, she felt she couldn't give any more. But when the attending midwife admonished her and warned her that the baby was in distress, Traudel gave her last efforts—it was finally accomplished. They had a scrawny-looking baby girl. They named her after an author, Karin Larsen. By the time they became parents, Jorgen Johannes Larsen and Johanna Gertraud Boden had been a couple for over three years. They met and fell in love in Lobau, a small German town located in the east of Saxony. Shortly after Jorgen was released from duly serving in the Danish Navy, he once again left Sallinge, his native village on the island of Fyn in Denmark. He arrived in Saxony by train, came to further his education with only a large suitcase in hand. The suitcase was won in a horse-racing event when he was a teen. Germany offered the latest and most innovative techniques in dairy production of milk, butter, and cheese.

Surprised by the question, when asked by government officials where he wanted to go, Jorgen had simply pointed with his finger to a random place on a large map of Germany, which covered most of an imposing wooden conference table. By pure chance, he found himself at the very plant where a beautiful redhead worked as bookkeeper in the front office. Although she didn't let on, because that was against her nature, Traudel was immediately drawn to the blond, tall, and handsome Dane, whom all the girls in the office swooned over. From the start, Jorgen made no secret of his admiration for the slim, attractive redhead. He even borrowed flowers, already arranged in a vase, that decorated the desk of another office girl, to place on Traudel's desk. A meticulous and conscientious worker, she always sat so primly in her starched white lab coat next to the window in her small office. Though her smile could light up her whole face, her temperament was of a more withdrawn nature. Less than a year after moving to Varnsdorf, they'd finally married. Their simple ceremony on November 13, 1943, was officiated early in the morning by the mayor. It was just the two of them at the old city hall, along with local officials, of course. Once they were pronounced man and wife, they'd caught the next train to Bischofswerda, Germany. This charming old German town, which dates back to 1227, was Traudel's birthplace. Much of her early childhood was spent in the care of her maternal grandparents. She grew up nestled securely within a large extended family who'd lived and worked in Bischofswerda for generations. On this special November Saturday, family anxiously awaited arrival of the newlyweds. Due to compulsory induction into German military, several of the men were away serving in the heinous war. Still, the wedding of Traudel and Jorgen was celebrated in grand style. A delicious feast was prepared consisting of rabbits roasted in real butter. Jorgen had smuggled across the border several pounds of this precious yellow commodity to share with his new family. And there was plenty of champagne to go around to keep the wedding party in jovial mood.

Both German and Czech was spoken in the quaint border town of my birth. In Varnsdorf, I spent little more than the first four years of my life. There were no roots in Czechoslovakia, no family relationships. By pulling a dining chair over to our kitchen window, I eagerly climbed up to have a look down the country road and across to the lovely tree-lined meadow. Quite regularly, colorful Gypsy caravans quietly settled in the meadow during the dark of night. That was what I was looking for.

Their intermittent presence in the meadow provided a sense of excitement to my early childhood. Occasionally, I was allowed to join the dark-haired Gypsy children for play. Though, mostly I just observed their comings and goings from our open kitchen window. Gypsies were discriminated against, and the caravans never stayed in one place for long.

One little girl's family stayed longer than was usual for these nomadic ethnic groups. This raised in me hope that she could always be my friend. Her hair was pitch-black, with loose curls falling down her back. My hair was nearly white, and there was precious little of it. Not yet three years old, my looks somewhat resembled that of a little boy. It didn't help that I was frequently dressed in pants. I wanted so much to look like my friend with her curly black hair.

Gypsies were dirty. So I was taught. I had noticed the mother had dirty fingernails. And her long gray skirt was stained. But she spoke so kindly to me. And she had very gently stroked my hair. I could tell she loved her daughter. She always treated her affectionately. I was confused about Gypsies. Once, on a warm and beautiful summer day, I stripped and romped naked in the meadow, running and playing with the rest of the children. But this was certainly not acceptable behavior for the kind of little girl I was supposed to grow up to be. Now, I only watched from my little perch by the kitchen window and longed to be with them.

Eventually, the devastation of WWII was over. No longer did we feel the terror that accompanied warnings over the radio of upcoming air raids, nor were we forced to quickly evacuate. Several times in my early life, my parents had frantically left home in search of a place of safety when evacuation orders were issued. After one such time, they walked home along the highway after an air raid was called off. The road and skies were clear, when in the distance a lone military plane appeared on the horizon. As it speedily approached, it suddenly swooped almost straight down toward them. Terrified, they pushed the stroller into the weed-filled ditch running along the highway. They feared the worst, as they tried to cover their infant child with their bodies. A gust of air swooped over them. Shaken and relieved, they watched until the plane disappeared over the horizon. It was an American combat plane, likely piloted by a frisky young officer who thoughtlessly had a little fun at the expense of locals. I was too young to remember these incidents. But I eagerly listened to stories told and retold through the years. On another occasion, my parents had returned home to find their small abode invaded in their absence. Soldiers had stolen what few valuables they found. The apartment was left in complete disarray, clothing all over the floor. The drawer of a lovely mahogany chest was emptied and pulled all the way out. A crass soldier had defecated into that drawer.

At one point the war brought tragic news all the way to the idyllic village of Sallinge in Denmark. My father's family had erroneously received information that their son and brother, his wife, and their baby girl lost their lives during an air raid.

One frightful day my parents unknowingly went from the frying pan into the fire. Years later my father penned the following narrative. He named it *An Angel Stood Guard*.

> Everything was chaos early morning on May 9, 1945, the day after Victory Day in Europe—the first day of freedom. I was in charge of dairy production at the factory. As milk is a daily necessity, I felt sure we could continue production. We soon learned differently.
>
> Troop after troop of Russian soldiers marched by. We were outside moving milk jugs, when suddenly a jeep careened to a screeching halt in front of our

building. Three officers jumped out. All were drunk, and proceeded to rob us of our watches, rings and money. It is no fun to be strip-searched with your back against a wall and a gun held to your chest by a very intoxicated officer.

After this frightening ordeal, my wife and I left our apartment. With baby and pram we made our way along a back road to the home of elderly friends. The Purmanns had cared for our wardrobe—washed and ironed our clothes for years. It was noon by the time we reached their place. By evening, it became apparent that we had gone from the frying pan into the fire. Russian soldiers swarmed everywhere. They had taken control of the army base located near the Purmann's neighborhood. And they had looted the local hotels and amassed huge amounts of alcohol for their consumption.

We spent the night, fully clothed, hiding in a small attic room. Volleys of gun shots accompanied horrendous screaming and hollering. Even machine-guns were going off. When would it be our turn? Towards morning I fell asleep. Eventually, all was quiet. Though, drunken soldiers had looted neighboring homes—molested women and children, and brutally murdered men, who valiantly tried to protect their families, none had caused any harm or disturbance in the Purmann home. Our precious friends had kept watch throughout the night. Soldiers had entered their home. But at no time did a soldier attempt more than a few steps up the stairway to the attic. My wife had prayed fervently throughout the long night. I am convinced, that Heavenly Father placed an angel as guard.

Even at fifteen months, I must have understood danger. I have been told that I made no sound throughout that long ordeal. I have no memory of hearing the raucous devastation caused by inebriated, marauding soldiers. But I do hold a clear memory of enduring a feeling of entrapment. And relief, when I was once again allowed to move freely where the sun's warming rays reached through evergreen pine trees.

WWII was over. But difficulty and unrest continued to be the order of many days. Frightening scenes often played out before us on that old curving country road. Etched into my memory is a bleak picture of untold numbers of men, women, and children leaving postwar Czechoslovakia through our border town. Many German citizens and people of German ancestry were expelled. Others fled from Eastern and Central European countries. Refugees were schlepping worn suitcases or pushing carts. Some were carrying their meager belongings tied into small bundles. All the while machinegun-toting Russian soldiers barked orders, even occasionally fired shots into the masses. I watched these sad individuals from my stool by the kitchen window and worried that my family might also have to leave. What would happen to my toys?

One dark night stands out in my memory. My father had finished reading me a bedtime story. Cradling my left hand in his large strong fist, he opened the door to the landing separating our living quarters from our only bedroom. My gaze was immediately drawn to an unusual sight down the sparsely lit stairway, where sprawled across the landing lay a naked woman. Her head was shorn, her white skin illuminated by the dim light in a small round window. Very abruptly my father pulled me into the bedroom and my mother hastily closed the bedroom door. The next morning, when Mother and I walked down those stairs to do our daily shopping, I asked for an explanation to the unusual sight from the night before, even showed Mother exactly how the woman lay sprawled across the landing. Though I employed all my three-year-old persuasive powers to extract the truth, Mother steadfastly maintained I had only dreamed this. But I knew what I had seen. It would be decades before I learned that women who were discovered to have fraternized with Nazi soldiers were stripped naked, and their heads were shorn.

On a sunny afternoon in September 1947, I begged my aunt to open the kitchen window. I was curious to see the big stork that had bitten my mother. But Tante Hilde wouldn't let me pull the dining chair over to the window. She insisted it wasn't safe. I tried my level best to assure her, that I was allowed to do this. Mother let me do it all the time. Frau Vanitec let me do it. I really wanted to see that stork. And though I didn't share this with my aunt, I wanted Frau Vanitec. My nanny was busy, however, tending to my mother. I'd overheard the adults talking among themselves. Frau Vanitec was tending to my mother so I could get to know my aunt.

Tante Hilde was my mother's eldest sister. I didn't know her well, and I was beginning to decide that I didn't like her very much. My aunt had taken command of our home. The smell of potatoes cooking on the stove permeated our small kitchen. Tante had boiled up big pots of water. The kitchen window was all fogged up. My mother's cries and moans were troubling me. At last, Tante Hilde opened the kitchen window. She allowed me to pull up my chair. I was just to have a quick look. But alas, it was too late. I had missed the stork that brought my baby brother. That mean stork had bitten my mother and caused her to cry out in pain. He was gone. Flew away before I succeeded in persuading my aunt to open the window.

For many months, my German-born mother had urged my father to arrange for our family to leave Czechoslovakia. My parents had lived and worked as expats in Czechoslovakia for more than five years. Mother wanted our family to go north, to my father's country. In Denmark, we would be far removed from the ravages of the recent war and from the evils of communism.

In May 1948, my family left comfortably on an airplane from Prague to Copenhagen. This was my second flight to Denmark. I was looking forward to the chewing gum, had gotten my first taste of gum when we visited my father's relatives in spring of '46. To keep my ears clear and free of pain, I was given instruction to chew the gum vigorously throughout the flight. Prior to our departure, my father had encountered governmental difficulties, because my mother was German. When he offered a bribe, he was given the necessary papers required for us to leave the country as a family. Thankfully, we left under much gentler circumstances than did the refugees I had so anxiously observed from our kitchen window in Varnsdorf. My parents had shipped ahead some of our furniture, as well as two sturdy wooden crates. Sadly, my favorite doll was too large to pack. Her arms and legs had moving joints. I loved her, but

I had to give her away. I was allowed to bring two smaller dolls. Their limbs were stiff. Their yellow hair painted on. I pretended to like them. And I knew my mother didn't much like my big doll with the long matted hair. Several precious tea sets were also given away. They were gifts from Uncle Helmut, my mother's eldest brother. He owned a porcelain factory in Dresden. Then, one fine day, he and his wife and two young children left behind their home and everything they owned. They flew to West Germany with only the belongings they could pack into two suitcases. Their freedom was more important than their possessions.

Chapter 12

At the age of four, I spoke both German and Czech but no Danish. This made me somewhat of a curiosity to local children. Several kind friends took me under their wings. My mother was fond of telling that I mastered Danish in just two months' time. She had observed how I tried speaking both German and Czech with the neighborhood children. When neither worked, I apparently resigned myself to my fate and went about learning a new language. Several Danish words continued to trip me up. It took a while before I could get my tongue around them. I owe much credit to my kind and inclusive neighborhood friends. A very sweet and sensitive young girl was nine years old. Patient and kind, she was eager to help me properly pronounce this new, strange vocabulary I was learning. She'd find me and sit me down on the lush green lawn in front of our yellow brick apartment building. Here, we rehearsed difficult Danish words until I could pronounce them properly. I looked forward to time with her. And I admired her blond curls. My hair was still short and impossibly thin and straight. My gentle friend had a visible handicap. The fingers on her left hand had failed to grow. I was a curious child, and her tiny baby fingers fascinated me. When I asked her about them, she chastised me for my curiosity.

Out of necessity, I became my mother's interpreter. She, of course, had the challenge of having to master this foreign Danish tongue just as I did. Though, there may have been times when Mother relied on her little interpreter a tad too much. I occasionally thought so. I was six that sunny summer day my mother took us children on a lengthy walk to buy discounted fresh eggs at a country farmhouse. I was to pay close attention to the way leading to the farmhouse. In the future, it would be my responsibility to make this weekly trip to buy eggs for our family. This worked the first time. The second time, I was sent away with a stern admonition—and no eggs. Mother went back to buying eggs at our local store. My mother was more reticent when it came to reaching out and making new friends. I would try to get her involved with the mothers of my young friends, but to no avail. She had encountered prejudice from a neighbor who lived in the upstairs apartment in Copenhagen! This once-friendly neighbor had assumed my mother was from Austria. When she realized her mistake, she never spoke to Mother again. My father thought he had the perfect solution. Mother should pretend to be from Austria. "Nonsense," was her response. "I'm from Germany. They might as well get used to it." To my knowledge, this is the only incident of prejudice my mother experienced in her new country. In spite of Nazi occupation of Denmark during WWII, Danes were generally forgiving and inclusive. In the early fifties, a number of Danish families opened their homes to German schoolchildren who were given the opportunity to spend summer vacation far removed from the destructive images of the recent war and the chaos of rebuilding their bombed-out cities.

For four months we lived with my father's aunt. Tante Ketty was divorced from my fraternal grandmother's younger brother. She was raising her two teenagers on her own. Her daughter, Lilly, was sixteen, and her son, Jorgen, fifteen.

One of the two wooden containers shipped from Varnsdorf never arrived. It was that crate which, among necessary items, held the few toys I was allowed to bring. Cousin Lilly kindly offered to make a new doll for me. She had very little money and purchased individual pieces for doll making from the local hobby shop. That was when I realized that Lilly must like me a little bit. She wasn't always very nice.

The doll project proved to be time-consuming. Before she could assemble the doll, Lilly had to paint facial features as well as paint each body part. Lilly made it quite clear that I was to stay away from the project until the doll was finished. The doll torso was made of soft white cloth, but head and limbs were fragile. They were porcelain.

It was hard for a little girl to wait. Finally the last pieces were painted. Two chubby legs were left on the windowsill to dry. This was the day Lilly was going to assemble my doll. I was beyond excited. But I was to wait till she got home from work. Cousin Jorgen warned me not to touch the legs. I just couldn't help myself. I had to pick up those chubby pink legs. I just wanted to feel them and admire them. I was surprised they could stand all by themselves. That's the way I left them when I went outside to play. It was a beautiful day. The sun was shining. The white lace curtain blew in and out of the open window with the breeze. Lilly found those chubby doll legs shattered on the floor. I wasn't entirely convinced that I was at fault. Though, I realized this was a distinct possibility. I should have left them alone. Jorgen had warned me. Lilly didn't pay much attention to me after that episode.

For much of her life, Mother regularly attended the Church of Jesus Christ of Latter-Day Saints. Unfortunately, the church had not been available in Varnsdorf. One afternoon, on a street in Copenhagen, she recognized two young men to be missionaries teaching the doctrine of her faith. Unable to speak Danish, she'd handed them our address on a crumbled piece of paper. Days later they showed up at Tante Ketty's apartment. Soon after that, Bernd and I started attending church in Copenhagen with our mother.

The same elderly sister was always at the piano. Careful not to get in her way, I stood quietly to her left. Her fingers moved nimbly over the keys. I had never seen crooked fingers like hers. I asked her about them. I was certain they must hurt. She explained that it didn't matter. She was still able to play the piano.

Cousin Jorgen was a kind and patient young teenager. He was also quite shy. I had a crush on him. Still, I couldn't bring myself to share my stick of gum with him. The two missionaries had brought me my first taste of Wrigley's chewing gum. With two sticks of gum in my hand, all I could spare was the tiniest corner for Jorgen. Actually, I managed to brake off two tiny corners. I was not yet five but well aware that I ought to have shared better. By fall, my family had moved to our own apartment. We now lived in Greve Stand, an idyllic beach town southwest of Copenhagen. When on a sunny afternoon Aunt Ketty and cousin Jorgen paid us a visit, Jorgen surprised me with a ring he'd made himself. Fashioned to look like a tiny silver belt, it was precious to me. Unfortunately, it was a bit too large, even for my middle finger, and I soon lost it. Jorgen promised to make me another ring. Though this one fit better, I lost that ring too. My friend and I tried to find it by retracing our steps. I prayed earnestly to find my ring—like the girl in a story I'd heard in Sunday School. But my prayers were not answered. Somehow, this was not a deterrent to my faith.

My father continued to seek better employment. I was six when my family moved to Skive, a small town up north by the fjord in Jutland. I was finally old enough to go to school. I loved learning, and I loved singing patriotic Danish songs. Then, one day, I came to the startling realization that I could never really belong in Denmark. What threw me off course were lyrics to an old Danish song written in 1850, by Denmark's famous storyteller, Hans Christian Andersen. It goes something like this: "I am born in Denmark. This is my home. My roots are here. My world started here…" By the tender age of seven, I had not yet understood that a good portion of my roots were solidly and deeply planted in my father's country.

Keenly aware that *my* world started in Czechoslovakia, I still remembered living there. On some days, I still longed for that time. I missed my nanny, Frau Vanitec. She had taught me the Czech alphabet and praised me for learning it quickly. When she and I had walked to and from her home, we regularly passed the tall building where children in Varnsdorf attended school. Directly across from the school was an imposing old church with a very tall steeple. Here, I fell off my sleigh and rolled onto the street, right in front of that church. It happened on a frigid winter's day, when snowflakes swirled in the air and painted my whole world white. Frau Vanitec had accidentally pulled my large wooden sleigh too close to the curb, and I was unceremoniously dumped off. I wasn't hurt, just startled. We giggled about that all the way to her house. I loved being with her. Quite often, I was allowed to go home with her to spend the night. She always removed her teeth and put them in a tall glass of water before going to bed. They sat on her nightstand until the next morning, when I would see her put them back into her mouth. I would get to do that when I grew old like her. Somehow, this did not impress me.

Quite regularly she took me to her church, where lovely candles flickered inside a dimly lit cavernous chapel. I would look up at impossibly high ceilings decorated with beautiful paintings. It was very crowded in her church. Most were older women in dark coats wearing kerchiefs, like Frau Vanitec.

Then arrived the defining day, when Frau Vanitec broke the news that my family was moving to Denmark. We were coming up to the school when I innocently asked her to tell me more about the things I would learn. This time, she seemed annoyed by my question. Said I should forget everything she taught me. I would have to learn all new letters to the Danish alphabet instead. Frau Vanitec seemed sad. I didn't understand, and it made me sad too. But I could tell by the way she talked about it that she was also annoyed. And I wondered if moving was not such a good thing. For a long time already I had looked forward to starting school in Varnsdorf, where children enrolled at age four. Frau Vanitec had promised to teach me how to read. Now, I wouldn't know anything, and that worried me. Longingly, I kept turning my head to look back at that beautiful building. I would never even get to go inside.

She was the grandmother I never had. I loved her very much. But I was never to see her again after we left Varnsdorf. She lived alone. Had no children. Her husband was serving time as a political prisoner. Perhaps this is why I, at such a young age, was aware that one's freedoms could be lost for small infractions or innocent mistakes. After moving our family from Skive to the charming coastal town of Grenaa, where we lived for several additional years, my parents finally settled in Odense. Located on the island of Fyn, Odense is the third largest city in Denmark and known for being the birthplace of famous nineteenth-century Danish author Hans Christian Andersen. We studied him in school. He and his tales are loved by Danish children, as well as children all over the world. *The Ugly Duckling* and *The Little Match Girl* are among his many famous fairy tales.

I was almost eleven by the time of this move. We now lived on the island of Fyn where my father was born and raised. My widowed grandfather, along with several of my father's siblings, still lived on this island with their families. There was the feeling of having settled down. It was comforting to have relatives living close. A whole new chapter in our lives. I enjoyed getting to know my Danish cousins and my aunts and uncles. Though, it wasn't always idyllic. Family relationships can be difficult, and for our family, it was no different. I was particularly excited for the opportunity to get better acquainted with my only living grandparent, my paternal grandfather, Hans Jorgen Larsen, whom we children addressed as *Bedstefar*. He had moved from Sallinge to Odense sometime after the passing of my grandmother. A quiet and humble man, Bedstefar had made his daily living carving wooden shoes for the farmers in the area around the village of Sallinge, where his ancestors had lived and worked for generations. He was also the village barber. Right next to their humble home, with the weather-darkened straw-thatched roof, was a workshop the size of a small garage. When farmers from the surrounding area needed a shave or a haircut, Bedstefar stopped carving shoes and took care of them. These two jobs afforded a modest living for his family of seven children.

It was commonly thought that Bedstefar was he first child born to his parents. The story we children grew up with was that our great-grandfather, Hans Erik Larsen, was once an affluent and influential man in his village—a man who had it all. The owner of the only grocery store in that area, he had built both the store and a spacious family home in Sallinge. Sadly, after many years of excessive drinking and gambling, he lost both his reputation and his wealth. Often there's more to family lore than meets the eye. Through FamilySearch, we now know that our great-grandfather was a widower, when at age twenty-five he married our great-grandmother, Maren Hansen, who was five years his senior. Their first child, born in 1885, the year Erik and Maren married, was in fact a daughter, whom they named Maren Christine. With no further information available on Maren, we can only assume that she died at birth. Our paradigm shifted to compassion for our great-grandfather. We are all so ill equipped to judge each other.

When he was only five years old, Bedstefar tumbled off a haystack and broke his leg. His shin developed two large open wounds that never healed. Throughout his life, his injured leg was treated daily with salve and covered with fresh gauze bindings. He used a cane and walked with a pronounced limp. Though we never once heard him complain, our grandfather most likely endured considerable pain. In his late sixties, it became necessary to amputate his bad leg above the knee. In spite of being fitted with an artificial wooden leg, my grandfather never learned to walk without the use of crutches. A man of few words, his eyes spoke the love he felt for his family. I was almost seventeen when we lost him. He died in late December—fifteen years earlier, on that very same date, my grandmother had also passed away. Uterine cancer took her life quite unexpectedly at the relatively young age of fifty-six.

I stood in her kitchen once. I was a young mother by then. More than twenty years had passed since her death. Looking through her large kitchen window, I could see an imposing tall and wide oak tree that was growing in the grass-covered side yard. I felt pretty sure that my grandmother's view through her kitchen window was the same view that I had in front of me. Oh, to have known this kind and gentle woman, who was born Ane Katrine Hansen. She gave birth to five sons and two daughters. She supplemented the family income by cooking and serving at dinner parties in their village and surrounding area. My father was the third child born to my grandparents. They suffered the loss of their second youngest child when he was only thirteen. Ernst became chronically ill, and his growth was stunted. It was said he suffered from *gulsot*, a condition that turns the skin yellow.

A meetinghouse had so recently been completed in Odense, and we soon began to regularly attend my mother's church. This opportunity had not always been available to us during our several moves. There were few congregations in Denmark and fewer meetinghouses at that particular time in history. Eventually, there were six of us in my immediate family. My brother, Carsten, was born in 1953, while we still lived in Grenaa. His birth was to have completed our family. It was a surprise, according to our parents, when little more than five years later my sister, Reni, joined our tribe.

Chapter 13

It was in Bischofswerda, Germany, that my maternal grandmother invited two American missionaries into her home. As representatives for the Church of Jesus Christ of Latter-Day Saints, these two young elders steadfastly taught her the principles of the restored gospel of Jesus Christ. She found this to be a gospel of happiness and of light and truth. It was a gospel of hope in an eternal future. It resonated with her.

As she faithfully studied and prayed, she gained for herself a strong testimony of the Book of Mormon. In late October of 1927, Emma Martha Bellack Sturm Boden became the very first person in Bischofswerda to be baptized. One year later, her three younger daughters were also baptized. My nine-year-old mother was her youngest child. It was Traudel who had opened the door to the missionaries the first time they ventured up the stairs to the family's apartment. Although, that first time the missionaries had not been welcomed inside.

A single mother to six children, my German grandmother had dreamed of immigrating to Salt Lake City with her family. Along with many other converts, she hoped to start a new life in Utah. Her dream never materialized, however. Perhaps because her three eldest children, a daughter and two sons, never joined the church.

Widowed during the First World War, my grandmother was left with five children to raise. Following this tragedy in her life, she married her high school sweetheart, who until then had remained a bachelor. Emil Gustav Max Boden was a toolmaker, almost forty, when he and Emma Martha were joined in marriage in 1918. My mother is the only child born to the two of them. Unfortunately, the marriage of my German grandparents did not last. The large family my grandfather married into proved too much for him to handle. Perhaps because he was a bachelor for too long, and he was raised an only child. Perhaps it was that several of my grandmother's children were uncooperative.

Sadly, after the divorce of her parents, my mother had very little contact with her father. I was playing with dolls on our living room floor in Skive the first time my mother shared the story of her father's one and only visit to her after the divorce. Emil had climbed the many stairs to the family's third-floor apartment. He was probably winded when he knocked on their door. Traudel was not yet three and that day had been unwilling to go with him. Her mother was at work, and her father was not invited inside to visit with her. Instead, he was chased right back down those many stairs by her two teenage brothers. One of the boys threatened him all the way down with a large butcher knife in hand. I was horrified to hear this unhappy tale. I was only six, and it left me thinking that my grandfather could hardly be blamed for not coming to see her after such a frightening incident. Mother wanted me to understand how very fortunate I was to have a father. My father was a wonderful and loving man. I adored him. He was the parent to comfort me if I was sad or upset or if I awoke in the middle of the night from a bad dream. He read stories to me. He taught me to read while we lay on the floor next to the heating element in our apartment. He was always the one to help me with my homework. He was tall and handsome. I thought he was the most handsome man compared to all other fathers of my friends. My father was my hero. My mother's older siblings had sadly taught her to feel only antipathy toward her own father. She was well into her later adult years before she finally internalized this. To my mother's recollection, she'd spent all but fifteen hours with her father after her parents' divorce. Their brief reunion must have occurred after she met my father. He remembered Emil as a pleasant enough elderly white-haired gentleman.

Both my maternal grandparents were gone before I was born. Neither of them ever married again. My grandmother was one of the many devastating casualties of the Nazi regime in Germany. Brought to the hospital with a high fever, she died two weeks before her sixty-second birthday. Aware of widespread "mercy killings" of sick or disabled elderly, she had warned her eldest daughter that were she to be hospitalized, she would not return alive. It was just one year and ten days following her death that my grandfather also passed away.

At the age of twenty-three, my mother had lost both her parents. As Emil's only child, it became her sole responsibility to arrange for his burial. None of her siblings felt enough compassion to lend a hand of support. Nor did any of them attend the services with her. Her father was laid to rest on a cold and foggy Christmas Eve in 1942.

My grandmother's dream became my dream. I am the second of Emma's grandchildren to immigrate to the United States of America. Eventually four of her twelve grandchildren all emigrated. Now, in the twenty-first century, a large posterity live in this country. How grateful I am for her choice to invite two young American missionaries into her home. How grateful I am that she chose to be baptized into the Church of Jesus Christ of Latter-Day Saints. The restored gospel of Jesus Christ has profoundly affected my own life journey. As I ventured far from home on my own, my faith became my strength. My faith was the one thing that remained a constant in my life. Already, from early childhood on, I knew that I could rely fully on my elder brother, my savior, and my redeemer, who is Jesus Christ.

Chapter 14

America

As I comfortably cruised across ocean and plains high above the earth, it was easy to think of myself as a modern-day pioneer. In Copenhagen, I had bid family and friends farewell before boarding a large and spacious silvery jet. I didn't know when I'd see my family again, but that thought was pushed straight out of my head. This was my adventure. I left green pastoral Denmark behind late on a sunny Friday afternoon. Left without fully understanding the emotional impact of also leaving behind family and friends and everything that was familiar. I was young and excited to be on this new adventure. My parents had ventured out in their youth. Now, it was my turn to head out into the world. To a new life and yet a new language to conquer, in sunny Southern California.

Even before the rising morning sun slowly spread her warm, orange glow above the horizon, my flight readied for landing in Los Angeles. Still illuminated by streetlights, the cities passing below seemed endless. Bright headlights identified what seemed like miniature cars that already crowded the myriad of freeways on that early Saturday morning on May 11, 1963. Awestruck, I pressed my forehead against the small oval window to my left. Neighborhood after neighborhood glided past. As the sun rose ever higher in the sky, millions of shimmering blue swimming pools winked up at me. Tall, stately palm trees swayed in the breeze. What an amazing first impression!

I was nineteen and seeking to experience a new life. For more than a year, I had waited anxiously to obtain my immigrant visa. That treasured document, along with my Danish passport, was safely tucked into my purse. A large x-ray of my chest was safely ensconced in an equally large mustard-colored manila envelope. This recent x-ray was also a required document. It proved that my lungs did not show symptoms of tuberculosis. With these three important documents in hand, I was allowed entrance into the United States of America at Los Angeles International Airport. I was a legal immigrant.

Coming to California truly proved to be an exciting adventure. But undeniably, there was the almost immediate feeling of culture shock. My mother was right. This was not going to be easy. Thankfully, it was my good fortune to be welcomed to Los Angeles by a wonderful and kind host family. Members of the Church of Jesus Christ of Latter-Day Saints, my host family, had sponsored me. Though I was a stranger, they welcomed me into their circle as one of their own. In my new ward, I was equally surrounded by friendly and welcoming church members. But it is a struggle to walk a whole new path in life, a struggle to learn a new language and to absorb and incorporate new and unfamiliar cultural norms. And of course, I missed my family. I missed them a lot. And I missed my friends in Denmark. I missed a thousand things from my former life. All that was familiar was a world away.

For five years I had studied English in school. Now, exposed to American slang, I found my language skills to be woefully inadequate. I could pretty well handle one-on-one conversations. But when several people joined the conversation, it might as well have been Greek for all I understood. Mispronunciations and misunderstandings tripped me up. Jokes went straight over my head. I often felt completely overwhelmed, woefully ignorant and inadequate. Occasionally, I thought about returning home, back to all that was familiar. Instead, I prayed for endurance and for help to conquer. A small English/Danish pocket dictionary, brought from Denmark, became my trusted companion. I started a pattern of learning and nurturing new words, not unlike a gardener tending her garden. I reminded myself that I would feel a whole lot better with a year under my belt. *Be patient, just give it one year.* That became my goal and my self-admonition, a kind of mantra. And somehow, that first year flew by. Surrounded by open hearts and helping hands, I grew to love my new country—beautiful America. Americans came from all corners of the world. Here I would grow my roots. I am eternally grateful for the love and kindness of my host family and of mostly everyone I met.

Little more than six years after my arrival, I became a naturalized citizen. It felt so right. I had never felt completely Danish. Nor was I completely German. There were no ancestral roots in the country of my birth. Czechoslovakia was simply the place where I was born. Never again, during my childhood, did we go back to visit the small town that was Varnsdorf. The borders to my birthplace were closed. Communism ruled in Eastern Europe, and communism was feared. Gradually, I settled into my new routine. I loved the climate in beautiful, sunny Southern California! Practically every morning revealed endless sunshine from a cloudless blue sky. This was so very different from the unpredictable weather pattern in Denmark. The frequently biting, cold wind and way too many rainy days in the country of my fraternal ancestors, who for generations lived under the arctic north, tried my patience from the beginning. Denmark is so beautiful, so full of vibrant colors when the sun shines. But in my father's country, the sun doesn't shine enough for my temperament. As if a nurturing sun was somehow offensive, steel gray and even white clouds gather regularly to block sunshine out. They form an oppressive dome which shields city and town from warming rays, sometimes for weeks on end. Coming or going from home, I often had to lean into a stiff and buffeting wind. Headwind when you left would be headwind when you returned. Summer or winter, it was the same. Just count on being bullied almost daily by a teasing Nordic wind.

Most Danes took the local weather pattern in stride. To me, the frequent rain and almost constant wind was unsettling. The summer after I turned thirteen was the absolute worst. Denmark stayed drizzly and cold for the entire summer vacation. Deep in my heart I was determined to leave this subarctic weather behind. Initially, I planned to go south. To live near my German relatives, where I could spend my life in a more hospitable environment. Several of my mother's siblings, as well as her close cousin, had settled in West Germany. My host family lived in a lovely home in the suburbs of Los Angeles. I felt blessed, counted myself so fortunate to have landed with this good and caring family. Dot and Hoagy owned a truck and transfer company in Los Angeles. Three weeks after my arrival, I was employed in the family business. I had so much to learn. Upon graduating high school, I worked as an apprentice in a law office in Odense for two out of a three-year apprenticeship. I was used to typing lengthy reports on old-fashioned typewriters, had learned typing and stenography by taking night classes after work. But sitting in front of an electric typewriter was something entirely new. For a good while, that very sensitive machine confounded me. Given an instruction manual to read, my eyes took in words that boggled my mind. Holy cow! (An expression I learned very early.) How was I going to do this? The day I received my first paycheck, I felt almost wealthy. Even after setting money aside for tithing, and after I paid Dot my weekly room and board, I had money left over. Determined to save enough for a trip home, I soon acquired a savings account. Before I left Denmark, my father made me this promise: "Karin, I will move heaven and earth to bring you back if at any time you decide you want to come home." I shall be forever grateful to my father for sending me off with such loving support.

For most of my childhood in Denmark, there was never much left over after bills were paid, and my parents had not wanted me to go. The first of their four children to leave the nest, I was spreading my wings to fly so very far away. Years later, a job in sales became my father's forte. This allowed my parents many opportunities to visit my family. They grew to love America. Spread over nineteen visits, my parents spent over two and one half years with us. My children were blessed to know and to love their Danish grandparents.

Dot and Hoagy were the parents of three sons and a daughter. Their eldest son was in Denmark serving a mission for our church. Aware that I had applied for a visa, he asked me to save a date for him upon his return. Silently jubilant, I agreed to this future date. But months went by, and I was unable to locate a sponsor. Without a sponsor, I would not be eligible for an entrance visa. To my delighted surprise, a letter arrived from his mother, Dot, inviting me to join their family in California. They were willing to sponsor me. As a final step in the visa qualification process, I was now able to make an appointment for an interview with the American Embassy in Copenhagen.

When I arrived at the embassy for my appointment, I was greeted by a solicitous American gentleman who inquired about my reason for wishing to immigrate. Was I planning to be married in Los Angeles? I explained quite truthfully that there was no such plan in place. I further shared with him that a certain young American man was currently in Denmark finishing the last year of a thirty-month mission for the Church of Jesus Christ of Latter-Day Saints. Though he and I had never discussed our mutual attraction, a girl is allowed to dream. I was not the kind of girl to make assumptions. Following the interview, this kind gentleman wished me well and walked me all the way to the street. Now, with the promise of an actual visa, I joyfully hailed a taxi back to the old Copenhagen central train station. Soon, my train rumbled on to one of the large ferry boats, which hourly crossed the waters of the Great Belt between Zealand and the smaller island of Fyn. I was so excited. It felt as if my journey to the other side of the world had already begun.

Until Hoagy helped me find my first car, for which I paid out of my savings, I hitched a ride to and from work with son number two. Bobby was a surfer and drove a black hearse. I was not entirely comfortable with this arrangement—these vehicles were used to transport dead people. We didn't play like that in Denmark. But such was the California style back in the sixties. Hearses proved a convenient way to carry surfboards. And California kids walked barefoot a lot, a strange sight for a girl from the arctic north. Though, it didn't take long before I copied that fashion in balmy Southern California.

Kenny was the youngest family member. He was a kind and quiet teen and already at fifteen a superb artist. Jana, the third child and the only daughter in the family, generously shared her spacious bedroom with me. Soon to be a junior in high school, Jana was an excellent dancer. She really had the moves down. She was a brown-eyed blonde, like me. Over summer of '63, we became the best of friends. Her parents always hoped she would have a sister. That was where I came in. Jana is my "American sis." She taught me much about life in my new country. I will be forever grateful to her and to this wonderful family I was so fortunate to be embraced by. On Sunday, June 2, 1963, exactly three weeks and one day after my arrival, a handsome, suntanned young man with sun-bleached hair made eyes at me throughout Sunday School. Seating in our classroom was arranged in a circle, and he was directly across from me. Not a member of my ward, he quickly introduced himself after the meeting came to a close. We chatted only briefly before I accepted his invitation to join him for a banana split at Baskin Robbins. That same afternoon, Nat King Cole's famous incandescent voice romanced through the sound system at the ice cream parlor: "That Sunday That Summer."

Over my first delicious banana split, I learned that Roger was a fighter pilot, stationed at the Naval Air Station at Point Mugu. The base was located up the coast in Ventura County north of Los Angeles. Roger flew F-4 Fighter jets and fired missiles. He was also a surfer. Together with his friend and surfing buddy, Hobie, Roger built his first surfboard himself while still in high school. They'd set up shop in the garage of his friend's home in Laguna Beach. Hobie's father had even lent Roger money for the materials needed. He and Hobie parted ways when Roger decided he'd better finish his education. A star football player at Laguna Beach High School, Roger had a full-ride football scholarship to USC.

A few years Roger's senior, Hobart Alter became a founding pioneer in the surfboard industry. As Hobie became more and more successful, Roger often wondered if he should have stayed in the surfboard-making business. Instead, he graduated four years later with a major in real estate and business from USC and immediately joined the United States Navy. One of only two officers selected out of about two hundred, Roger eventually headed out for flight training in Newport, Rhode Island.

After our first date, Roger immediately became a regular at our weekly church meetings for young adults. When M-Men and Gleaners planned an outing to Griffith Observatory in Los Angeles, Roger joined us. That evening at the observatory, while gazing at a trillion and more stars twinkling from the darkened sky of our breathtaking universe, he suddenly put his arms around my waist and swung me around. When he put me down, he leaned close and whispered into my ear, "I'm going to marry you." I chose not to respond to this rather startling remark. We hardly knew each other. Besides, I had other thoughts about whom I wanted to marry. But soon we were dating weekly, though not exclusively. That came months later. I was getting to know other young men as well.

No doubt there was a certain flair to Roger's courting. I had to admit that I enjoyed spending time with him. That is, until I learned that he had not been completely truthful with me.

Because I guesstimated his age to be several years younger, I was surprised to learn that Roger was twenty-seven. Curious to learn why he was still single, I asked him if he had ever proposed to a girl. When he merely answered no to my question, I took that answer at face value. Weeks later, Roger came clean. Over a steak dinner, at a restaurant in Laguna Beach, he brought up the subject. I listened to him explain that someone had proposed to him, and he had accepted. I was floored. To my further consternation, I learned he was the father of a six-year-old son and a five-year-old daughter. The children lived with their mother and grandmother. He was divorced for about two years. The marriage had lasted almost five years. For two of those years, he was intermittently at sea.

Roger defended his obvious deception with a question, "Would you have gone out with me again, had I disclosed this when we first met?" Somehow, I could not argue with the man's logic, but it was disturbing. It never occurred to me that he had been married. And I didn't appreciate being lied to. I didn't hesitate to tell him so. Prejudice told me I should not go out with him again. But when Roger called a week later, I accepted his invitation. I had missed him. I always experienced a feeling of peace when we were together, and we always had a good time. He was patient and kind. Early in our friendship, Roger had introduced me to Laguna Beach, a beautiful, romantic coastal town south of Los Angeles, where he grew up.

Born in Riverside, California, his family moved to the coast before his teenage years. On my first visit to Laguna Beach, Roger introduced me to his sweet mother, Lola. He also introduced me to an eccentric older vagabond known to locals as the Greeter of Laguna Beach. With his gray beard, long straggly hair, and very friendly attitude, Larsen was a well-known fixture to all who called Laguna Beach home, and he was from Denmark.

Frequently, Roger would show up unannounced in our ward on Sundays and quietly slip in next to me during Sacrament meeting. We regularly attended Sunday evening firesides in Huntington Beach together. On dates, we often drove to Laguna Beach, where we went swimming in the ocean or walked barefoot on the beach. Occasionally, we surfed. Or went bicycling. Then off to the movies after a full day. One Saturday afternoon at the beach, Roger gave me his surfboard to use. I was to paddle out beyond the rocks at Emerald Bay and hang there while he dove for crab and abalone. At first Roger swam next to me, his diving tank strapped to his back. Beyond the rocks, he disappeared. I bobbed lazily on the surfboard while taking in the beauty of the surrounding environs. The ocean was perfectly still that afternoon. The sky was cloudless, a brilliant blue. Homes seemed to hang suspended from the bluff above the beach. I imagined being up there, taking in the amazing view over the ocean. Life seemed perfect on this beautiful, warm, and sunny day. But I was getting worried. Roger was gone for a long time. When he finally surfaced, he brought up an enormous spider-like king crab, which he nonchalantly placed in a net on my surfboard. Then, he was gone again, out of sight for a very long time. When he surfaced again, he brought up abalone. Later that evening, we boiled up dinner at his sister's house.

When Roger introduced me to Solvang, a quaint Danish town located a couple hour's drive north of Los Angeles, I got to eat a favorite Danish cuisine and bask in the familiar, touristy as it was. One evening we took off from a small Orange County airport. High above the earth, we skimmed lightly across magnificent ripples of clouds strikingly painted the color of flamingos by the evening sunset. Ever higher we soared in a two-person orange Beechcraft T-34, a Navy trainer. Bouncing from cloud to cloud, it was as if we were alone in a world of our own. It was magical. Occasionally, we touched on the subject of marriage. Basically shared our hopes and expectations for the future. It was always casual conversation. I was in no hurry to be married, and I told him so. I had feelings for another. Yet feelings of mutual affection were slowly beginning to blossom.

Chapter 15

Friday, October 11, started out as any normal day. But it proved anything but a normal day. By mid-morning, I was surprised to receive a phone call from Roger. He'd never called at the office before, and he'd sounded strange when he said he needed to come and see me. When Roger arrived at the house that evening, I was home alone. He walked in the door and immediately picked me up and swung me around twice. "Let's go eat," he suggested. "Then we can talk."

When he finished what he came to tell me, I couldn't eat. There had been an accident. The mother of his two young children had died. She and a boy-friend had collided with a train in Orange County sometime after midnight. Both were gone instantly. Now, that he would have the sole responsibility for raising his two young children, Roger wanted to know if I could ever consider marrying him. With a look of pleading in his eyes, he sat so earnestly before me. I was completely overwhelmed and deeply shaken by this sudden unimaginable tragedy. It was simply too much for me to even consider. I was still only nineteen.

When he called again, Roger promised not to mention marriage. We were to go out for a quiet, casual time together. That night we dined at a favorite oceanside restaurant in Long Beach. Another time we went deep-sea fishing. I caught four fish. He caught none. Eventually, Roger suggested we take the children to a football game at his alma mater. I knew this was coming. How could it not? It was the first time I would met his children. It had been difficult to keep this very tragic situation out of my mind. I thought about it daily. My heart went out to his young children who now lived with Roger's older brother, Grant, and his family. In their short lives, they had already experienced a home with contention leading to divorce. Now, the death of a parent and a new home living with relatives. The children were darling. We had a pleasant time at the ballgame that afternoon. I weighed the possibility of a future together. But I simply could not see how this relationship could work. I was so young to be mother to two growing children.

Weeks later we ran into each other at a Thanksgiving dance in Huntington Beach. We did not speak but snuck long glances over the shoulders of our respective dates. Only days later Roger called again. A thought entered my mind. *You will marry him if you continue to go out with him.* This thought made me think I should not accept his invitation. But I did not follow my own counsel. Soon, we were again seeing each other every week. Now, I told myself to ignore Roger's incessant "marry me." At the same time, however, I began to seriously weigh our relationship. We got along well. We seemed compatible. I felt peace when we were together. We never really had disagreements or problems. Other couples from our young adult group were getting engaged and planning marriage. Still, there was his past. And it was disturbing to me. No young girl grows up with the dream of marrying a divorced father with two children. Furthermore, it was a huge responsibility and frightening. But as the oldest child in my family, I was used to younger children. I started asking myself, "How hard can it be?"

At five, Stacy was just a few weeks older than my little sister. A vivacious little blond girl, she reminded me of myself as a young child. When we'd stop to visit, she always came running to me for a big hug. That first time, when Roger had brought the children along to the ballgame, Stacy had climbed into my lap and happily announced, "My mommy died. But my daddy is going to get me a new one." Mark had been guarded most of that day, quite the opposite of his eighteen-month younger sister. He was quietly observing. Wasn't immediately ready to get close and cuddle up. Eventually, though, he too decided he wanted affection. Suddenly, at the end of that first day we all spent together, Mark asked, "When is it my turn to have arms around me?" Roger and his mother had both shared with me that Mark was a difficult child. I remember thinking that this little boy's early environment might have a lot to do with this. He probably just needed a stable and loving home. My two younger brothers were easygoing, obedient boys. They'd never caused major problems. How hard could it be?

And then, on the evening of March 11, when Roger again chanted, "Marry me," I answered, "Okay, I will." The look on his face as he turned to me was one of disbelief. Roger stopped his car, got out, and danced around the dark, deserted neighborhood. Then he got back in the car and drove until he found a phone booth. He called his mother to share the news. We both spoke with her. She sounded so pleased. I was touched by how happy Roger was. "Let's get married soon," he suggested. The children could stay with their uncle and aunt until they started school in the fall. It would give us time to adjust. That made sense. But I suddenly felt completely overwhelmed. It was like I had agreed to marry not just one but three. And just possibly, that was going to be harder than I imagined. I thought about telling him that I needed more time to think about this. That maybe I couldn't marry him after all. I really struggled with the conflict between my feelings for Roger and my worry that I was taking on more than I could handle.

The San Francisco Bay Area became our honeymoon destination. I was given a lovely wedding shower. Ken, at fifteen, had artfully constructed an impressive replica of the Golden Gate bridge, which served as decor. Dot and her friend Lois made my wedding dress, and Dot had stitched by hand a sequined blouse for me to wear under my sky blue wedding suit, which had a white mink collar. I totally splurged on that suit because Dot and I both decided I had to have it. The fit was perfect. We'd spent a whole day in Los Angeles shopping for my trousseau at Dot's favorite department store, Bullocks. By the end of that day, I had mostly depleted my savings. Helpful and kind, Dot had guided me along and made everything work smoothly for me. She counseled me somewhat about marriage. "The dishes aren't going anywhere," she suggested. Then added that I was always welcome to visit her if I needed to talk. However, she would send me back home at night to sleep in my own bed.

The last Sunday before our wedding, I was standing on their deck in Laguna Beach with Roger's father. Having arrived home from church minutes before, we were quietly gazing over the magnificent Pacific Ocean as it stretched in its vast blue splendor before us. My soon-to-be father-in-law, Jedediah, was a quiet man. He hailed from original Mormon stock. One of his ancestors, Gilbert Belnap, had served as bodyguard to Joseph Smith, the first prophet of this dispensation. Earlier in his life, Jedediah had been a heavy smoker. When he became severely ill with emphysema, a tracheostomy was performed to facilitate his breathing. Now, to speak audibly, Jedediah needed to place a finger over the opening of the catheter that was permanently implanted in his throat. Each time he spoke, he paused intermittently to get air. This made me wonder if he was quiet by nature or by necessity. He and I had never really had much of a conversation. He turned to me.

"Karin—you'll never have to worry—about Roger taking good of you—financially.—He's a very hard worker."

The year was 1964. I appreciated my future father-in-law's concern to let me know that I would be well taken care of. I was certainly prepared to do my best. And I had prayed much to know if marrying Roger was the right decision. But frankly, I wasn't entirely sure I had received an answer. I always felt a strong sense of peace when Roger and I were together. I was going by that. Surely, God would not let me have this reassuring feeling of peace if I was making a wrong decision.

The day before our wedding turned out anything but peaceful. First on our agenda was my doctor's appointment to get a blood test. Then on to Los Angeles for lunch and to pick up our marriage license. In 1964, a blood test was required documentation for a California marriage license. Roger was more than an hour late to pick me up. That was a new one. But stuff happens. And that day, stuff kept right on happening. At the doctor's office, we waited longer than expected. Then, we stopped at a phone booth so Roger could place an important phone call. At last, we were on our way to a late lunch in Los Angeles. Lunch was about over the same time Roger realized he'd left documentation for his own blood test back in the car. He'd tucked it into a thick white envelope containing other important documents.

But there was no white envelope in the car. Now worried, he realized he must have left the envelope in the phone booth when he placed his call. Trying to quell our panic, we were once again on the busy freeway. It would take at least thirty minutes to make this round trip. Our panic only increased when we located the phone booth and there was no envelope! What to do now? We called Dot at her office, and Roger explained our predicament. Calm and helpful, she directed him to a Los Angeles clinic in the vicinity of the county recorder. One could walk in for a blood test without an appointment. No immediate parking place was available when again we arrived downtown. Time was running out. Roger decided to sprint to the doctor's office. I saw him turn the corner. Within minutes I had a parking place.

It was hot that day. Worried and confused, I rolled down all the windows. My heart was beating fast. *Was this how God was answering my prayers? Was he, at this late moment, letting me know that my decision to marry Roger was a mistake? Was God giving me an out?* The wedding was less than twenty-four hours away. Roger's out-of-town family were flying in that evening. I couldn't just drive away and leave him stranded in LA. Nor could I walk all that way back. I honestly considered both options. From where I parked, I could see a tattered, dirty vagrant shuffle over to a dented garbage can. His hair was disheveled. Looked like it was weeks since he had a bath. I'd never seen the likes of this in Denmark. Distracted from my own problems, I watched him lean into the dirty garbage can and rummage through the contents. When he came up with a half-eaten apple, he hungrily finished it off. *Why, God? Why is this poor soul eating out of a garbage can, and why do I sit in a hot car wondering if I am supposed to get married tomorrow?* I wanted to scream, *Why is that?*

Suddenly, standing by the driver's side was my triumphant fiancé. Sweat was dripping from his face unto my left arm resting in the open window. Roger had made it back in record time. "Move over." He grinned and let out a relieved sigh. "We're going to make it."

I never shared with Roger that I'd thought of running away. And that wasn't the only time this thought occurred to me. Only this time, I wondered if he too might have had second thoughts. It seemed as if unseen forces were at work to keep this union from happening.

On Friday, May 15, 1964, Roger Gaylord Belnap and I were married in the Los Angeles California Temple. In the city of Santa Monica, we were sealed "for time and for all eternity." As we quietly waited in the sacred and majestic Los Angeles temple with our wedding guests, it hit me—*No one from my own family is here with me on this important day.* In 1964, it wasn't financially possible for my parents to afford the trip. I understood that and choked back insistent tears. Suddenly, the ceremony was over. And just as suddenly, my tears spilled freely. I stood sobbing in front of the whole wedding party. Perhaps it was the many changes I'd encountered during the past year.

So much in my life still seemed new and unfamiliar. And I hadn't been able to look forward to my marriage to Roger without worry and conflicting thoughts. Most often it felt completely overwhelming, that I'd soon be a mother, or rather a stepmother, as well as a new bride. That is not the dream of a young girl. And of course, no one from my very own tribe was with me on this important day.

My new husband looked bewildered. But Roger took it in stride. He held me close and did what he could to dry my tears.

Chapter 16

Before we started house hunting, I came to realize that Roger's heart was set on finding a house he could fix up in his spare time. I couldn't imagine living with the mess of a fixer-upper. He tried to convince me. Carefully, I explained to Roger that I was willing to become an instant mother, but our home could not be a construction zone, at least not indoors. Thankfully, my husband had the tolerance to hear me. His savings were just enough for the required down payment on a small, newly constructed four-bedroom home with two baths on Coe Street in Camarillo.

In 1964, Camarillo was a sleepy, small town amid wide open fields of agriculture. I soon became familiar with shopping at the Navy Commissary and Exchange. The first time I ventured on base to shop on my own, a steel-gray Navy jet thundered down directly in front of my car. I had not realized that the landing strip began immediately to the right of the highway. Nor had I noticed or heard the jet as it came in for landing on my left. I tried my best to prepare for childrearing by reading Dr. Spock's best-seller, *Baby and Child Care*. Since our engagement, I had read and learned during my lunch hour. The thick softcover book was stored in the glove compartment of my 1956 lime-green Chevy. One day a guy from work borrowed my car to run an errand. Apparently, he felt the need to snoop in my glove compartment. Back at the office, he'd approached my colleague, Jonny, asked her in a hushed voice, "Is Karin pregnant?" This was beyond embarrassing to me. Jonny knew my situation, but I had neglected to mention at the office that I would become an instant mother when I married. I was struggling with sharing the instant mother part. It was a different time from the social problems of the twenty-first century. Today our family would fit right in with what is modern life in many American families. But in 1964, our family situation was outside the norm! From the very beginning, though, my life has seemed destined to be lived outside the norm.

It was still summer when the kids joined us, and I often headed to the beach with them. We'd stop at a local convenience store to buy our favorite orange-flavored ice cream pushups. I had not yet learned of the dangers associated with excessive sunbathing and took great delight in sitting in my beach chair, soaking up the sun. I looked in wonder at Mark and Stacy playing in the sand. I marveled that I was married. I was a mother. How did this all happen to my life?

Very quickly I learned that being a big sister is a cakewalk compared to being a mother 24-7. But I too was resilient. And I had the full support of my husband. A new family was created, and there was much love to go around. For a while, at least, our family seemed complete. We felt it wise to establish a comfortable routine for the four of us before adding a new baby. The children needed stability and lots of love. I could give them that. Though I had a difficult time with their frequent squabbles. Contention of any kind was always a sore point with me. In charge of my own destiny, I was planning for a life without contention. I was young and idealistic. I soon learned that it was not at all realistic to expect life to be smooth. We made frequent weekend trips to Laguna Beach, where we had the luxury of time alone, while the kids were with their cousins. But these travels also revealed one of the major differences between Roger and myself. We were polar opposites when it came to timeliness.

While growing up in Denmark, everyone in my family did his and her level best to be ready at the agreed-upon hour. This seemed the *fair* way to do things. To my surprise, my husband had a different philosophy regarding time. He could not be hurried. He was never late for work. That was not an issue. I'd be packed up and have the kids ready to leave for the drive south, only to find my husband in the garage fixing something or other that suddenly seemed important. It never failed. After all, weekends were leisure time. Inevitably, two hours passed before he was ready. I did the math. I could be frustrated, or I could choose to adjust my attitude and expectation. If we had previously agreed to leave at 6:00 p.m. on a Friday night after work, I planned to be ready by 8:00 p.m. Somehow, that worked. The Serenity

Prayer always resonated so strongly with me. "God, grant me the serenity to accept the things I cannot change, the courage to change the things I can, and the wisdom to know the difference."

By fall I broached the subject of my seeking work outside the home. I had too much time on my hands. Usually, by early morning, my house was in order. I needed more to do. The kids were gone until midafternoon. "But I don't want my wife to work." This was my husband's initial response. In the sixties it was customary for the little woman to stay at home. I had no objection to the job title for women during that particular time in history, but I was bored as *housewife*. I enjoyed knitting and needlepoint in my spare time, but only for so long. TV was never that interesting to me.

Soon after, Roger learned that Point Mugu was hiring civilians for office work on base. Perhaps I could be hired for part-time work? My plan was to go to Point Mugu for a job application directly from my dental appointment.

As Dr. Wells and I engaged in the customary small talk, he learned of my plan to seek employment. "If you're looking for a job, I have a test for you to take," he quickly offered. I was hired while still sitting in the dental chair for my appointment. I knew absolutely nothing about dentistry and hesitated to accept. But Dr. Wells assured me, "I will teach you my way to assist."

This was the beginning of my dental career. For almost a year, I worked as a dental assistant five mornings a week. Though I nearly passed out on my first day while assisting with the extraction of seven teeth, I soon felt confident in my new job. My interest in dental hygiene was naturally piqued. Early in our relationship, Roger had shown me around the campus of his alma mater. As we strolled past the dental department at USC, Roger had casually pointed out that dental hygiene was the perfect career choice for a woman. The wife of one of his good friends was a registered dental hygienist. She worked only a couple of days a week. They had a young family. Oh, to have the opportunity to study dental hygiene. That very day I'd tucked the tiniest seed of that wish into my heart.

Chapter 17

A reserve officer in the Navy, my husband eventually felt he needed to be a commissioned officer in order to continue serving. When his application for a commission was denied, Roger turned in his resignation. A strong feeling of patriotism and pride in our country accompanied our experience while at Pt. Mugu. However, this was during the Vietnam War. Several of Roger's squadron members were MIA. Others had lost their lives. It seemed a fortunate time to get out. By the time of his release in 1965, Roger had served seven and a half years in the US Navy. Flying was his passion, and Roger seriously considered becoming a commercial pilot. Already, he had passed the intensive test required to fly for a domestic airline. But it was to be a waiting game. There was a hiring freeze. By pure chance, Roger fell into a sales job with a young insurance company.

It was a surprise when the Navy unexpectedly came through with his commission only weeks before he was due to become a civilian. But by then my husband had grown excited about his new career opportunity. Quickly he'd moved to the top of the sales force, where he and two fellow agents vied for the weekly position of top producer. My husband won awards as well as prizes and vacation trips. Awarded Rookie of the Year, we celebrated during a long convention weekend in San Diego. Soon, Roger decided to make the insurance business his permanent career choice. His father was absolutely right. Roger was a diligent and dedicated worker. No longer was his job nine to five. His new job required self-motivation, something my husband possessed in abundance. He could work without stopping and often without sleep.

Less than a year after leaving the Navy, we moved into a beautiful five-bedroom home in Santa Barbara, a move that considerably lessened Roger's daily commute. Santa Barbara was idyllic. Through our kitchen window was a spectacular view of the Santa Ynez Mountains. Solvang, that quaint Danish village Roger had brought me to shortly after we met, was less than an hour's drive away. It was a slice of Denmark to enjoy and an opportunity to sample foods I missed. It was often a lovely Sunday afternoon excursion for our family.

Our first baby was born nearly three years after we married. I had already suffered two miscarriages, and even this pregnancy proved a challenge. I was six months along before my obstetrician offered even a glimmer of hope. "I consider this to be a miracle, Karin," he'd finally said. Kenneth Roger Belnap was born at 2:11p.m. on Monday, April 3 in 1967. Love filled my heart nearly to bursting as I gazed into my newborn son's little face. My soul was filled with joy and gratitude. I could scarcely believe he was mine.

But the experience of entering this world had not been easy for our little one. Deep indentations were imprinted on his skull where the forceps gripped tight. Black and blue marks streaked across both cheeks. Even his left ear was black and blue and still scrunched up from the forceps delivery. My baby boy had been in deep transverse arrest. At that time, children were not allowed in the hospital rooms, nor were they allowed physical contact with the newborns. Mark was ten, and Stacy was almost nine. They were able to view their baby brother only through the windows of the nursery. We seemed to very nicely settle into being a family of five, when one day, before leaving for work, my good husband hinted: "If I use baby lotion, do you think you can pay attention to me too?" My ears heard clearly my husband's words. But my heart did not hear him—at least not that day. He made no sense. My time was not my own. My husband, and even our two older kids, could do much for themselves. What was *wrong* with him? Eventually, I figured it out.

By July Roger was assigned to work about two hours down the coast. The kids had summer vacation. There was no reason we couldn't all head to the beach. We locked up our home in Santa Barbara and moved to a furnished retro apartment located across the beach in Malibu. Appliances were from the forties! But it was clean. We anticipated living at the beach for a couple of months. The previous summer we'd spent a month living up north in Cayucos. Located along State Route 1, Cayucos was a quaint beach town in San Luis Obispo County. Everything in Cayucos was old. It seemed we lived in a time warp. Malibu was more interesting. Time seemed to fly while we lived at the beach. Nat King Cole's cheerful rendition of "Roll Out Those Lazy Hazy Crazy Days of Summer" played regularly over our sound system. To me, each and every day was like summer. As a youth, I could only dream of living in such temperate climate. I loved it.

Chapter 18

While in Malibu, Roger received a phone call that would again change the course of our lives. Family Life Insurance Company needed a new account executive in Arizona. They were offering this position to the new Rookie of the Year. A few days later, we found ourselves on a commercial flight from Los Angeles to Phoenix. It was early August. The blast of hot air that greeted us in Phoenix that early evening, was beyond anything I imagined. Welcomed at the airport by a company executive and his wife, we were immediately brought to a casually elegant restaurant for our evening meal. The Cork and Cleaver was to become our favorite place to eat for many years to come. It was the early days of open salad bars, and this restaurant offered the best. As we learned more about the job proposal, my husband got more and more excited. The next couple of days became a flurry of activity. As broad daylight revealed a better look at the dry desert environs, my somewhat hesitant excitement began to wear off. A good wife supports her husband in his career endeavors. I got that. But as the desert heat intensified with each passing hour of every day, I became less and less enchanted with the prospect of moving to this inferno that was Phoenix. Arizona was so completely different from the beautiful, green, lush, and vibrant state of California I had grown to love. There was no ocean. There was one freeway. Everything in this state moved at a slower pace. That dreadful dull brown color was everywhere. Downtown Phoenix was old, dilapidated, and dead.

One month later, however, five Belnaps rolled into Phoenix early September 1967. To this day I maintain that I was dragged to Arizona by the hair. We came from three fun-filled days on the Colorado River. The warm river water was ideal for boating, waterskiing, and swimming. We'd had a blast with Roger's brother and his family. Now, it was time to buckle down and get our family at least somewhat settled in the rental home we'd secured in the foothills of Squaw Peak. We discovered this newer neighborhood at the end of a long, hot day during our August visit to Phoenix. Several lots were available, and we'd decided to build. Admittedly, there was a certain excitement to this new and different part of the world. One early evening, an enormous brown dust cloud approached. Huge and menacing, it hovered like a dense brown mountain seemingly ready to engulf our whole neighborhood. Minutes later, debris and dust swirled through the air, while trees bowed to fierce blowing forces. Just as suddenly, the blue sky reigned again. This was our introduction to Arizona dust storms—intense weather fronts that intermittently roil across the arid desert. By the end of September, the heat turned down, and the weather became absolutely delightful. It didn't take long to discover Lake Saguaro for boating and water skiing. Only an hour's drive from our home, this lovely desert lake became a frequent and favorite playground for our family.

On December 9, 1969, our son John Luke Belnap came into the world at Good Samaritan Hospital in Phoenix. Our second baby boy had two distinctive features—a rather prominent nose and a deep dimple in his chin. It was not immediately apparent that this baby boy would grow up to become a very handsome man. Labor was short and relatively easy. We were over the moon. Each baby is a true miracle. I felt such deep gratitude, love, and joy for the privilege to be a mother.

John-John was three months old when my parents visited for the first time. I had traveled to Denmark twice since arriving in America, but I longed for my family to experience this new life I had found in my adopted country.

An amusing incident occurred while my parents were home alone with our children. Fully potty trained, Kenny called his grandmother to come and help. She didn't quite understand what he needed and responded, "Not now, Kenny." Determined to get the help he needed, he went to her and pointed repeatedly to his little bare behind while demanding, "Yes, Grandma. Now!" Kenny was a precocious child. His verbal skills were amazing. When he was barely older than two, he had recited the Pledge of Allegiance for all the sisters in Relief Society.

Among many local excursions, we'd planned a driving trip to Salt Lake City. Roger and Mark stayed home to hold down the fort, while three adults, two eleven-year-old girls, and two little boys headed out in our packed station wagon. My sister, Reni, had accompanied my parents on this trip, and she and Stacy became the best of friends. Reni took great delight in being aunt to Mark and Stacy.

Close to the Arizona/Utah border, we stopped to sample Indian fry bread, where dusty Indian villages dotted the landscape with tepees and round hogan dwellings belonging to the Navajo natives. Mangy dogs and beautiful dark-haired children played in the dirt, much as children do everywhere in the world. The culture and desert landscape was so very different from the flat agricultural land of Denmark.

My parents and the girls were to spend a few days with close friends from Denmark, who immigrated to Utah more than a decade earlier. My little boys and I drove to Sandy to spend the next few days with my Danish friend and her family.

Reunited and heading back to Arizona, my mother regaled me with fresh news of friends and acquaintances—all former members of our Danish branch. One had studied to become a dental hygienist. On that long drive home, my own dream occupied my mind. But it was an impossible wish. I had long ago laid to rest any desire to pursue a career. We had four children. My having a job was not a financial necessity for our family. I owed my time to raising our children. I was doing what I loved. But it would have been wonderful to have had this opportunity. To have the security of a profession! Late that night, while telling Roger about our trip, I admitted, "I wish, I had a career like that." Little did I know that this impossible wish of mine was about to become reality. When Roger came home from work the next day, he brought with him an application to Phoenix College. He'd spent a portion of his day researching the only dental hygiene program available in our area at that time. His excitement was apparent as he shared with me what he'd learned.

Completely unprepared for this development, I was reluctant to agree. I could not see how Roger's plan could ever work. Not with four kids. Not with a tiny baby and a preschool child to care for. But my good husband seemed to be on a mission. After seven years together, I should have learned to never underestimate his powers of persuasion. Every argument from me was met with a reasonable counter. Roger was totally prepared to cover for me. He even offered, "If you want to pursue medical school, I'm very fine with being a house husband."

Only weeks later I started summer school at Phoenix College. That first day, as my memory took me back to 1963, I walked from the parking lot to my English class with trepidation. That long ago fall, I had started classes at Cerritos College in Norwalk, California, and dropped them after only five weeks, having needed time to acquire a better understanding of my new language. Now, with several additional years under my belt, this was different. That early

June morning in 1970, I left class knowing I could do this. Roger was ready to leave for the office the minute I arrived. And I had to concede that Daddy at home early morning was as important as having Mommy at home.

Over the next three years, I made it through the premed curriculum by signing up for one class each semester. All but one prerequisite was left when I finally applied to the dental hygiene program. This two-year program was competitive. Phoenix College received over two hundred applications yearly. Only twenty-four students were selected for each fall semester. I took it in stride when I was accepted as fifth alternate. It was a lucky day, when less than two weeks before the start of 1973 fall semester, a slot opened. It was mine, if I wanted it. Did I ever! Now the end was in sight. But new arrangements would have to be made for our little boys. For the next two years, I would be in clinic all day on Tuesdays and Thursdays. The remainder of the week I had classes at Phoenix College until noon. My husband, of course, had his own work to see to, both at the office and in the field.

"Two years will fly by." Our elderly clinic dentist repeated these words time and again to our 1975 graduating class. And he was right. Two years flew by.

Suddenly, I had my diploma in hand. It was a stunning feeling to have realized my goal. What started as the tiniest seed of an impossible dream had come true. As registered dental hygienist, or RDH, I was licensed to practice dental hygiene in the state of Arizona. My loving husband was the one to thank for my career opportunity. Selflessly he'd given me an invaluable gift. And Roger never faltered. For five years he helped me, encouraged me, and smoothed the road for me as much as was possible. I was beyond grateful. Neither of us had any way of knowing just how invaluable this gift was to become.

As one of two graduating seniors, I was invited to join the Phoenix College dental faculty as junior clinic instructor. Flattered by this proposal, I allowed pride to rule and accepted the position. Though not without first talking this over with my husband, who chose to not persuade me one way or the other. As it turned out, for me and for my family, this teaching position was a mistake. In my heart I already knew I had accepted this job against my better judgment. Things started to unravel at home after two months. We'd never considered that I should work full-time. When I came home from work, I still had to prepare for the following day. Pretty soon, no one was happy. With less than a month left before the end of fall semester in 1975, I sat down with our clinic director and explained my need to make a change. And I shared with him our happy news. Our baby was due in early May.

"How soon would you like to leave?" Doctor asked.

Without hesitation I stated, "If I had my choice, I'd walk out of here today and not return."

His facial expression registered surprise. He had not expected this from me. How fortuitous that he had someone in the wings begging for a position within the dental department! If I wanted out of my contract, I was free to go. I was ever so grateful for his support and grateful that I had been forthright in stating my need.

Late that afternoon, I walked out of the Maricopa County dental clinic in downtown Phoenix for the last time. For the cost of only $1 per visit, many of our patients had little other opportunity for affordable dental care. As a student, I had enjoyed learning my trade and serving in this clinic, but as a teacher, not so much. I had purposely chosen a profession where I can give my work days to my patients and my evenings to my family. It was high time to return home after work and be done with it. This new chapter in our lives was celebrated at a favorite Mexican restaurant. Order was soon restored. Time was past due for me to assume all my duties at home.

Chapter 19

Several changes to our lives occurred simultaneous with my studies. William, the owner of a single-engine four-passenger Mooney Ranger advertised for partners, and Roger jumped at the chance to be part owner. He'd long held the dream to own his own airplane. Now, every fifth week, this small plane was his to use. I could only muster hesitant excitement for this new development.

William was also the owner of a helicopter. When he decided to sell this large mechanical bird to an out-of-state buyer, William hired a young man from our ward to follow along in his truck to the destination where the helicopter was to be delivered. Carefully, he tracked William, who was flying slightly ahead along the freeway. Somewhere in Texas, this young man watched in horror as the helicopter suddenly became tangled in power lines. As fiery darts shot out like firecrackers, the helicopter came crashing down. This was a devastating blow to our entire ward family. It was difficult to imagine what his widow was going through. Early that evening, my husband and I arrived at their home to offer our condolences. We found William's cousin and his wife, also part owners of the airplane, already visiting with Nancy. That night we joined the three of them for dinner at a local Mexican dive. Our hearts were broken for William's young widow, who was left with four children to raise. She barely ate. We barely ate. There wasn't much anyone could say. All rang hollow, in face of that day's tragic event.

Nancy had four young sons. Her two older boys, both younger than ten, were dropped off at the local public swimming pool that morning. Unfortunately, with news of the accident, no one yet thought to bring them home. One of their young friends found the two boys in the swimming pool, and she told them about the accident. With summer temperatures in Phoenix soaring over one hundred degrees Fahrenheit, two frightened young boys walked all that way home in the heat. Surely in disbelief, and still nurturing hope, they came thundering into the house while calling to their mother, "Mom... Daddy didn't die in the helicopter? He didn't die, did he, Mom?" Six weeks later tragedy struck again. William's cousin and his wife had invited friends to join them for a weekend trip in the Mooney. The two couples flew to Nogales, Mexico, to do some shopping. Upon leaving Nogales, the plane struggled to become airborne. A hundred feet in the air, it suddenly took a deep nosedive. It crashed a short way off the runway. According to NTSB, the airplane was packed with more weight in the tail end than could be safely sustained in the air. Nine children, ages two to ten, were orphaned in this tragic accident.

It had been our week to use the Mooney. William's cousin had arranged with Roger to trade weeks. It was terrifying to consider that it could have been my family in that plane.

On a lark we decided to sell our new home in north Phoenix. We'd lived there for only three years. Real estate prizes had shot up in the years since our arrival. Roger was eligible for a veteran's loan, and he wanted to invest in rental properties. With the sale of our home, he would be able to actualize this plan. However, with a veteran's loan, our family would be required to live on the property for a minimum of six months. I wasn't super excited by this prospect but agreed that six months was doable. When our home sold within a few weeks, we immediately moved to an available rental home in our neighborhood.

My brother, Bernd, had come to live with us from Denmark. Before a year was up, my soon-to-be sister-in-law also arrived. By then we occupied two of the four small apartments that Roger had subcontracted. To connect the two units, he had opened a passage through the adjoining kitchens. All eight of us squeezed into a combined space under 1,300 square feet. Toward the end of seven months, the walls began to crowd in on me.

To build our next home, we'd purchased a lot on a steep hill. The view west over the valley was breathtaking. But the more I thought about living there, the more uncomfortable I became. There was only room for a small backyard. Where would our children play? Furthermore, it would take almost a year to build. I wasn't sure my sanity could sustain another year with so many of us crowded into small quarters. A temporary move would give us time to think, as well as get us out of the apartments with the least amount of disruption to our family. Though we already had architectural plans completed, we agreed to postpone building. Before two weeks were up, we purchased an existing home on Squaw Peak, with beautiful views of the top of the mountain. Nestled, as we were, within the mountains, it proved a most quiet and peaceful place to live. The hum from city streets below never reached us. We took delight in watching colorful hang gliders as they quietly came soaring from the heights above. Come summer, we blasted for our first pool. It was exciting to follow the daily progress. Every year in Arizona, children lose their lives to drowning. Though our children knew how to swim, we added a fence. I had full lifesaving instructions posted inside kitchen cabinets and in our bathrooms. In case of an emergency, I was always fully prepared.

As much as possible, our family still escaped to Laguna Beach. Occasionally, we took our ski boat to Catalina Island to spend a night or two. After one such trip, we were surprised to suddenly be motoring home on a still and glasslike ocean. It was early in the morning. No wind and zero waves as far as eyes could see. Suddenly a school of dolphins surrounded us. These playful gray marine mammals rose out of the ocean while gracefully performing their distinctive dives. Silvery flying fish glided alongside us like birds. It was an unexpected and exciting natural water show. Sometime after our move to Arizona, Roger's father had approached him about moving our family back to California. My father-in-law would soon need a new real estate broker for the office he owned on PCH in Laguna Beach. He suggested Roger take that position. It was certainly tempting, and we considered it carefully. In the end, we chose to stay in Arizona. We both felt we needed to stay where we had landed. Though, I was somewhat surprised by myself. I missed California. Here was our chance to go back.

Admittedly, much had changed in Southern California. In the late sixties the beautiful beaches and idyllic local streets in Laguna Beach literally crowded with long-haired hippies. Openly, they smoked pot. Mingled among them were strangely shorn members of the Hare Krishna faith. Dressed in their long orange devotional robes, we could observe them walking up and down Forest Avenue while loudly chanting mantras. For a time this crowded spectacle even interrupted our trips to the local Baskin Robbins. Phoenix appeared to have the healthier environment for bringing up our children.

This was also the summer when our John suddenly became quite ill. His temperature was slightly elevated, and our family physician noticed swollen lymph nodes in John's neck. Frightening words, like leukemia and Hodgkin's lymphoma, were spoken by our doctor. It became a summer of weekly appointments and tests. When John's kidneys and liver enlarged, we were referred to a hematologist. Thankfully, this specialist spoke only words of comfort to two frightened parents.

"You have a perfectly healthy little boy," he assured us. Even before John was examined by this specialist, it became clear that our little boy's energy levels were improving. When Roger shared that John was given a healing blessing, the doctor knowingly nodded. "I'm not surprised."

In microbiology lab that same summer, I noticed the tiniest cut on my left middle finger. I had obviously nicked myself with the thin cover glass used with the microscope. That day we'd worked to identify unknown bacteria. By evening my finger was swollen and throbbing. Overnight, the size of my finger nearly doubled. White lines made their way up my left arm. All this because of the tiniest cut and unknown microbes working their mischief. At the doctor's office, I was immediately given an injection of penicillin. Unfortunately, this soon presented yet another concern. Within two days my torso was covered in an itchy, angry-looking rash. As a young child I had been severely ill with scarlet fever and was given daily penicillin injections. Exposed to this lifesaving medication, I had obviously developed sensitivity to penicillin.

Less than two weeks before Christmas came a surprise phone call from my father. Having just closed on a large sale, he wanted to know if he could fly the family to Arizona for Christmas. That afternoon, I fairly danced through Safeway while shopping for groceries. For the first time in ten years, my entire family would celebrate Christmas together. Bernd and Marianne had married in the spring and lived close-by. My hope was always that my family would one day be able to visit fairly regularly, in spite of worldwide distances. This was now happening. A dream come true for me and for my family. Less than a year had passed since I traveled solo to Denmark for a brief visit. Several months later my brother Carsten joined us in Arizona, along with a friend. We'd had such a great time with them, often boating at Saguaro Lake. Even spent several days camping and waterskiing at Lake Powell.

Right after I graduated in 1975, my husband signed up for a real estate investment seminar and invited me to come along to evaluate the opportunity. Soon, he decided to leave the insurance business for good. Roger had already obtained his license to become a real estate broker and soon signed on with a real estate company selling forty acre parcels of land. When his company merged with a popular local homebuilder, Roger became the in-house broker. He drove long distances when meeting clients to view land parcels. Each commute inevitably stretched over two or three days. Soon, the subject came up of once again owning an airplane. With access to an airplane, he would be able to fly clients to view properties in the early morning and return that same day. I wasn't super excited about this. I could never quite dismiss a nagging tinge of apprehension, but I agreed to my husband's plan to sell the apartments in order to fund the purchase of an airplane.

A portion of the proceeds was delegated to the purchase of a slightly used single-engine six-passenger Cessna 210. Roger's next plan included locating a lot where to build a sixplex and to find an investment partner. Over time we decided not to build the home we had made plans for on Squaw Peak. Roger allowed that his heart ached the day we signed the contract to sell our lot. We sold for double our purchase price. Quite happy with our good fortune, we would eventually learn that had we waited a year to sell, we could have quadrupled our earnings. Lot prices on the mountains in Maricopa County were suddenly exploding, and we had a prime view lot. I was grateful that Roger never again mentioned it. We put the experience behind us and purchased a large lot at the base of the Phoenix Mountain range. Located south of Shea and west of Tatum Boulevard, this area as well as the desert further north was still largely undeveloped in 1975.

Chapter 20

My parents visited once again but stayed only four weeks as my father needed to get back to his church service. He had joined the church in the midsixties and, less than a year later, was called to be branch president. He came to love his small congregation. In turn, was much loved by them. He served for more than seven years, with an additional five years as bishop of Odense Ward. When in his seventies, he was once again called to serve as bishop. He considered the many years he was privileged to serve to be some of the best years of his life. As a young man growing up in the small village of Sallinge, his mother had often lamented, "I wish we could afford to properly educate you, Johannes. You ought to study to become a priest." He had a way of cutting to the essence of what was important. Tall and handsome, he was also thoughtful, loving, and kind. She'd recognized in her son a special gift in the way he related to others.

Though my father was not a member of our church during my childhood, my parents regularly attended Sunday evening Sacrament meetings! This may well have served as their date night, as I was left home to look after my two younger brothers. Only occasionally did my mother attend Sunday School. She wasn't keeping the Word of Wisdom, a health code which eliminates coffee, tea, alcohol, and tobacco from the Mormon diet. She never smoked, but she enjoyed her daily coffee. And she willingly partook of alcohol if this was served at a party. Baptized as a child, my mother remembered this ceremony as a frightening occasion. In 1928, baptisms in Germany were performed under a shroud of evening darkness. The black, murky water of the Elbe River in Dresden had seemed terribly threatening to her as a nine-year-old girl.

The Evangelical Lutheran Church of Denmark is a state religion. Beautiful old churches are sprinkled throughout the Danish countryside. Even then, few Danes attend church. It is not past them to poke fun at regular churchgoers. While I was in my early teens, several families from our congregation immigrated to Salt Lake City. This left no girls my own age in our small branch. I mostly felt alone in church and out of place. Still, my mother insisted that I attend Sunday School and take along my brother Bernd. Eventually, I rebelled. She must have then realized the importance of being the example for our family, for she began to attend Sunday School and took along Bernd and Carsten. I stayed home, though not entirely due to rebellion or stubbornness! Deep down I wanted to go to church. I felt such peace there. Already, as a young child I had a strong testimony of Jesus Christ. But with no friends my own age to associate with, and without parental support while at church, it was difficult for me. On top of that, I had missed the opportunity to share with my new class-mates, when I switched schools, that I attended the Church of Jesus Christ of Latter-Day Saints.

Many of my new classmates lived in the more affluent neighborhood, where our church build-ing was located. Hoping not to run into my peers, I felt like such a fraud. It simply became too pain-ful. I knew the Lord knew that I didn't want to be seen or recognized. I always knew I'd be back. Even before graduating high school, I brought along some of my friends. As I matured, I cared less about what my friends thought. I wanted to share the blessings of the gospel and share about the strength I derived from regularly attending our meetings.

The day after my parents left to fly home, I learned that my baby was breech. My sister-in-law, Glenny, brought up alarming concerns and urged me to request a C-section. Her friend had given birth to a child born with the cord wrapped around her neck. Deprived of oxygen, during the more difficult breech delivery, this now twelve-year-old girl was mentally handicapped. After listening to this tragic outcome, I did not hesitate to bring up the option of a C-section. Roger's left arm was still in a cast. He had sustained a fall on a small incline while surveying an empty lot in our neighborhood and spent two days as in-pa-tient in Good Samaritan Hospital because his injury required surgery to remove a fractured lateral epicon-dyle. Only rarely had Roger been ill. Suddenly, he slept for hours. Somewhat overwhelmed, we felt we were getting hit with one thing after another. Now the emergency C-section. On top of that, laryngitis got my husband every time I started labor. For days Roger could speak only in a whisper. One other time, only, had he come down with laryngitis. It was that week in 1965 when he trained with Family Life Insurance Co. When the financial future of our family would soon be entirely dependent upon his sales performance.

Our daughter, Leslie Anne, was delivered the morning of Saturday, May 8, 1976. My husband walked by my side as I was wheeled out of post-op. "She's so beautiful," he whispered while leaning over my gurney. It was the day before Mother's Day. Immense gratitude flooded my heart for my healthy newborn child. My baby girl was so lovely, the best Mother's Day present ever.

Dr. Lawrence somberly admitted, "The cord was wrapped around her neck four times. Had we attempted breech delivery, she might not have lived, or she would have been severely retarded." A sobering thought, indeed. It seemed we had another miracle. We were incredibly grateful that Glenny had raised her concerns. Dr. Lawrence had not been immediately convinced that a C-section was necessary.

The following day a young Hispanic mother was brought to the empty bed in my hospital room. She'd delivered her firstborn child by C-section, and both mother and son were stressed from a difficult, lengthy birth. Barely was Maria settled before she was bombarded with visits from parents, aunts, uncles—absolutely everyone. Fortunately, that soon came to a halt. The nurses saw to that. It was immediately apparent that both Maria and her husband were intellectually challenged. Particularly Barry, who, in a loud, raspy voice, kept insisting to his wife that she did *not* have a C-section. With this commotion rocking my formerly tranquil room, I was trying to decide if I should feel annoyed or entertained.

Aside from experiencing an insensitive nurse in post-op, I was treated with care during my five-day stay in the hospital. Not so for Maria! The veiled rudeness and plain unkindness coming her way was disturbing. Maria had prescribed bed rest. Her baby, while in an incubator, could not be brought to our room. Promises to take her to the nursery in a wheelchair never materialized. Nurses muttered insults under their breaths about people who ought not be allowed to have children. If I heard this, surely, so did Maria. Admittedly, I harbored my own judgmental thoughts. Maria and Barry were unquestionably different. But she wasn't pestering the nurses. She meekly asked for help where she couldn't help herself. Eventually, I did what I wished I'd had sense to do much earlier. Over Maria's objections, I located a wheelchair. Undiscovered, I proceeded to push her into the hallway. Almost immediately two nurses came running. At last Maria was transported to the nursery. Of course, I knew I shouldn't be pushing a wheelchair so soon after a C-section. Plaintively, Maria thanked me. "I'm not used to kindness," she admitted. Sadly, this sweet and simple soul was perfectly aware that most people treated her indifferently. It is a sad fact that it is often the weakest among us who are bullied or treated unkindly.

At eleven years of age, I was admitted to Children's Hospital in Odense for atrial fibrillation. Here, I met twelve-year-old Lydia. She'd had no visitors for nearly three weeks she'd already spent in the hospital due to an intestinal disorder. Lydia and I became instant friends. In fact, in spite of varying ages, all five of us girls in that hospital room became friends.

That changed dramatically the second and final week of my stay. Like a swift and buffeting wind, Sonja swept into the empty hospital bed by the window opposite mine. Thirteen going on nineteen, she was immediately in charge. Daily pandemonium entered what had been a relatively peaceful hospital room. When no nurse was present, Sonja regaled us with inappropriate stories, even threats. In the presence of adults, Sonja's voice fairly dripped with honey. After lights were out on Saturday night, the atmosphere in our room became particularly demeaning. Though none of us escaped her sarcasm, Lydia was repeatedly singled out. It was difficult not to laugh at Sonja's antics, because she was a natural comedian. Then, suddenly Lydia broke. She burrowed deep under her comforter. As this lonely girl's anguished sobs rose through the goose feathers, all fell silent. In the darkness we listened to her heartbreak. That night, in the darkened hospital room next to Lydia, I determined to no longer be a participant. Not even by my silence. I prayed for courage to be a true friend.

Sunday morning dawned a brisk and sunny day. Most children in this hospital were ambulatory. Two nurses were assigned to take a group of us to a nearby park. The walk in the fresh air and the sunshine would do us good. There was a playground among the trees. I had apologized to Lydia. We walked behind the two nurses, purposely lagged a distance behind. Several of the girls were on the merry-go-round with Sonja. The ride was spinning lazily as we approached.

"Come on, Karin," they beckoned. When I didn't respond, they whispered among themselves. In a somewhat demanding tone, they called out again. Three remorseless girls now faced us on the nearly stationary merry-go-round. I stood there nervously with Lydia by my side. My eleven-year-old heart pounded insistently against my ribcage. I wanted to speak. But I had no words. I stared into their faces and slowly shook my head from side to side. To my astonishment, this simple gesture stopped it. Better yet, the next morning, Sonja was no longer in our room with us.

Chapter 21

My boys adored their little sister. We were all in love with our little girl. John, who had not wanted to relinquish his position as youngest child in our family, changed his attitude the first time he held his little sister. It was a sweet time in our lives—watching our children grow. Leslie's bright smile greeted me each morning as I walked into her nursery. She was like a little ray of sunshine. Raising my little daughter made me want to strive to be a better person.

Soon, I was expecting again. My babies would be less than two years apart. In 1963, when I first arrived in this country, I was amazed by the close birth order and the number of children in many American families. I marveled at mothers managing three to five youngsters all under the age of seven. The norm in Denmark during the fifties and early sixties was a couple of kids per family. Children were generally spaced several years apart.

Our perfectly healthy baby boy Jedd Joseph surprised us five weeks early. He was delivered by C-section on Friday, February 24, 1978. In spite of his early arrival, our son weighed in at six pounds, six ounces. Recovery was much easier this time. I had guessed we would have another little boy. We were thrilled. The birth of each of my babies are among my life's most cherished moments. My heart was so full of joy.

Chapter 22

Leslie very naturally assumed the role of second mother to her younger brother. She was not yet three when she came into the kitchen carrying Jeddie. His diaper had slid down, and most of his little pale bum was showing. My helpful daughter proudly announced, "Mommy, you don't have to get off the phone. I have already changed Jeddie's diaper." I'd heard lively chatter coming from the nursery but stayed on the phone. Those were the days when we were tethered to the wall when making phone calls.

The three of us regularly snuggled in my bed before bedtime. "Put your head on my shoulder, Mother," my young daughter often encouraged me while I read stories to them before bed.

The day before Kenny's fifteenth birthday, Leslie came into the kitchen carrying a long multicolored stuffed toy snake and a roll of birthday wrapping paper. "I'm going to give this snake back to my brother for his birthday." Kenny had given the snake to her. It was gifted to him by a friend. Later, to Leslie's disappointment, Ken took it back. My clever five-year-old daughter decided it was fair to gift the snake back to her older brother for his birthday. We all had a good laugh, including the birthday boy.

Jeddie adored his big sis. One afternoon I came into the kitchen and found him standing on the counter. Leslie was handing glasses and plates to him. "Look, Mommy, we're cooperating like on Sesame Street." They beamed. Their daily chore was to put away only the utensils. They were a team. Though at times they'd get into little tiffs about who was going to sit on my lap. I always assured them, I had one lap for each of them.

This was a busy time in our lives. Our children were growing up. Summer vacation was right around the corner. I wasn't ready as summer of 1982 approached. In the past, I'd always looked forward to our more relaxed summer schedule. Somehow, this year was different. I wanted everything to stay the way it was. As the end of the school year inched ever closer, I even recorded this in my journal: "I'm not ready for summer this year. I want everything to stay the way it is." I didn't know it was the beginning of the end of our lives.

Chapter 23

Quite familiar with the route to Jack in the Box, my yellow vista cruiser pulled up to the window. I'd promised a strawberry shake. Earlier that morning, the little kids and I signed up Leslie for a summer school cooking class at Cherokee Elementary. She was beyond excited. Already a busy little girl, Leslie was also taking ballet lessons. And since the age of three, she'd been part of a song-and-dance group. Soon, she was going to start piano lessons. Between my daughter's schedule and the schedules of her two older brothers, it seemed I spent a considerable portion of my days chauffeuring kids from place to place.

We'd recently celebrated Leslie's sixth birthday.

"Leslie Annie, you're growing up so well," I said, scooping her up with a big birthday hug. Her eyes brimmed with tears as she looked at me.

"Oh… Mother!"

A few days before her birthday, a seven-year-old boy new to our neighborhood had joined their regular foursome at the neighbors for play. Leslie had returned home all excited. "He kissed me, Mother." Taken aback, I gently cautioned her that she needed to wait till she was older and wiser. I hadn't scolded her. But my admonition clearly upset her. She'd put her arms up in exasperation. "But, Mother, I didn't know. You need to teach me these things." My heart had ached a little bit. My bright and helpful little girl was growing up too fast.

We finished our strawberry shakes. I was eager to get home and read a book I'd recently purchased. The book was written by Grant von Harrison, *Drawing on the Powers of Heaven*. That little book had lit an amazing fire in my soul. It reminded me of a Sunday morning back in 1980, when a returned missionary testified to our congregation, "There's power in reading the *Book of Mormon* daily." The young man's sincere words had penetrated my heart that day. I wanted and needed power in my life. For some time already, I was experiencing strange and unsettling feelings.

My youngest son was unusually pensive on our drive to Olan Mills photography studio. Jeddie had missed picture day at Kachina Country Day School. "Penny for your thoughts" elicited no response from my youngest son. Instead, he turned to me with a faint smile. His green stuffed dinosaur was in his lap. It went everywhere with him. He was dressed in navy-blue dress pants and a white polo shirt, his Sunday outfit for church. Jeddie had recently picked out the polo shirt himself and reminded me, "Now I just need a polo tie." When I explained that a knit-ted polo shirt was not worn with a tie, he was fine with that. It had made me smile. Apparently, I had a little clotheshorse on my hands. Earlier that morning, Jeddie had come in from the yard with a serious expression and asked, "Mommy, is it okay to kneel down by the swing set to pray?" When I assured him that it was okay to pray anywhere, his handsome face lit up in a relieved smile. He'd opened his dirty little fist with an offering of crimson clover buds with less than an inch of stems attached. I'd made a delighted fuss over his thoughtful gift and offered up a silent prayer of gratitude for my amazing little boy.

This youngest son of mine wanted to grow up fast. Eager to keep up with his older siblings, he often reminded us, "I'm not a baby." Two days of pre-school was not enough for this little man, and we had decided to let him have his way. Jedd was already signed up for full-time preschool come fall semester.

To celebrate the beginning of summer vacation, we took the kids to Lake Saguaro for a day trip. We packed lunch and snacks and stopped at a nearby grocery store to pick up drinks. Roger had come back to the car with a large plastic windmill—a sunflower. "A flower for you, honey," he'd offered with a kiss. We'd beached for the day at a favorite spot along the shore of Lake Saguaro. Jeddie had gathered a handful of seashells for me. It was a lovely, relaxing day of swimming, waterskiing, and fishing. Until I became alarmed by my two older boys' encounter with a rattlesnake. They had killed it.

At home I placed my sunflower in the planter surrounding our patio. It was in clear view from the kitchen window. I watched it spin in the gentle breeze.

With school out, the leaders and youth of our ward planned several days of camping and waterskiing at Lake Powell. Kenny had a prior commitment and would not be able to leave with the group. Rather than have him miss out on this fun excursion, his father arranged with one of the youth leaders to pick Kenny up at Wahweap Marina Thursday afternoon. They'd finalized the arrangement after Priesthood meeting. On our way home, we decided to make this short flight a family excursion with dinner in Page before the return flight to Phoenix.

That Sunday my heart felt the warm glow from two compliments. "Your family is so beautiful," said Stake President Shumway as we shook hands after Sacrament meeting. My kids must have behaved. My family usually sat on the second pew in clear view of the podium. On our way home, we stopped by our pharmacy to pick up a prescription. The kids and I waited outside by the car. A smiling gentleman on his way to the pharmacy walked all the way over to where we stood and exclaimed, "Your family is so beautiful."

By Tuesday I had changed my mind about flying to Page. I'd have to cancel my Thursday afternoon patients to make it work. When John heard I wasn't going, he opted out as well. The little kids were excited to go. This would be their first flight without me in the plane.

Wednesday, June 2, seemed unbearably hot. I had several errands that day and another long drive to the bookstore. By the time we got there, the kids were asleep in the back of the station wagon. I parked in front of the store and left the car running. Minutes later I was back. Two blond heads were visible through the back window. They must have awakened when I closed the car door. One of their storybooks was ripped to pieces. Illustrated pages lay scattered all around them. They'd had a disagreement, and Jeddie tore the book apart. This was not at all like him. For a split second I had the thought to give his rear end a swat, to emphasize that this was unacceptable behavior. *Don't!* This strong, clear message registered in my consciousness. At home, Jeddie followed me to my bedroom. "Mommy, I need you." My little boy looked up at me with a most forlorn look on his precious face. I scooped him up and carried him to the family room sofa. The two of us plonked down amid pillows and just cuddled for a while.

Thursday morning, June 3, no one was stirring when I quietly let myself out of the house for the ten-minute drive to my office. I couldn't recall a morning when the kids were not already up. My kids were early risers, always awake to kiss me goodbye. Except for this morning. Last night had gotten quite late. That's why I chose not to wake them. This would be a busy day for my husband. He'd be chauffeuring children to several different locations before starting his own day at his office. Thoughts of my family continued to scroll through my head while I drove.

The morning went by fast. My first afternoon patient was a no-show. So was the doc's. Surprisingly, the remainder of our afternoon cancelled within the hour. This was certainly unusual. The decision was made to close the office. On the drive home, I thought about catching up on my lack of sleep. The house would be quiet. By the time I rolled onto our driveway, I could barely wait for a quick nap. To my surprise, Roger's car was in the garage. I found him in the kitchen loading snacks and drinks into a brown grocery bag. The group at Lake Powell had left behind an electric generator. Roger had agreed to bring the generator to them. He was running late. He looked relieved when I'd walked in and said, "Will you get the little ones from the sitter, while I pick up Kenny? Have them cleaned up and ready when I get back."

Just like that my expected nap hung in the balance. Words formed in my head. *It's a thirty-minute roundtrip for me to bring them back here, and you'll be going right past the sitter's house on your way to the airport.* Strange how these words never reached my tongue. I answered agreeably and was out the door before he was.

I found Leslie and Jeddie outside in the hot June sun with the other children. Their faces looked flushed and tired. They begged for a strawberry shake. I didn't think we should take the time but promised them ice cream at home. Both were excited to be going along on this flight. At home Leslie immediately brought out a light jacket for herself and for her little brother. We'd purchased these cute little jackets only days before. She was eager for an occasion to wear her shiny pink one. It was hot in Page, just like in Phoenix. They wouldn't need jackets. "We'll take them along to California next time we go, honey," I explained.

My two blond darlings scrambled into chairs by the kitchen table. I opened a can of peaches and heaped a generous portion on top of three bowls of vanilla ice cream. For the longest time we sat around the table laughing and chatting and being silly. My love for my children burned strong. These two bright and vivacious youngest children gave us so much joy. But it was getting late. I reminded them that Daddy would soon be home. They needed to wash their hands again and put on the clean shirts I had laid out for them. Then, John arrived home. I dished out more ice cream and peaches.

Our faithful black cockapoo, Cookie, lifted her head and let out a soft *ruff*, an obvious signal that Roger had pulled into the garage. Moments later the kitchen door swung open. Kenny came hurrying through. His father, right behind him, called out, "Kids…time to go to the bathroom. We're in a hurry." Everything happened in a flurry of activity, and suddenly my babies were already in the car. *Hey, wait*—they knew not to leave the house without giving Mommy a hug and a kiss. But this afternoon everything was happening so fast. Perhaps that's why I thought, *Let them go.*

I watched my husband slowly back his car out of the garage. I blew kisses and waved. They all waved back. I could see two blond heads bobbing up and down in the back seat. The kids were so excited to go. Roger backed his car around to the left about the same time my right hand reached for the automatic garage door button. A thought popped into my head, *Maybe I should have gone after all.* That thought was dismissed as quickly as it entered, and before Roger pulled the car forward through our circular driveway, the closing garage door blocked them from my view. There was still time for a short nap.

I had promised John a shopping trip and called out that I'd be ready to go in half an hour. Then, I grabbed an outdated copy of *The Ensign*. The last thing I read before briefly dozing off was a reference to 137:10 in Doctrine and Covenants: "And I also beheld that all children who die before they arrive at the years of accountability are saved in the celestial kingdom of heaven." I made a mental note to include this scripture in my next Relief Society lesson, which was on baptism.

It was almost five o'clock that sunny June afternoon, when John and I headed to our favorite Scottsdale restaurant. John was an easy child. His needs at times squeezed between his more demanding older brother and his still needy younger siblings. It was so easy to focus on the needs of the other three when this child was so quietly unassuming. At age twelve, John was helpful and reliable. Had stepped right up to the plate when he became a big brother. More recently he'd taken over Kenny's job of mowing our front and back lawns. He also mowed our neighbor's lawns. And John and his dad had secured yet an additional lawn mowing job the week before school was out. They'd gone around the neighborhood together and found this extra job to keep John busy during summer vacation. It was on to the mall after our meal. John didn't like any of the pants he tried on. We'd already been to a couple stores. Out of the blue I was overcome by an overwhelming feeling of fatigue. It was almost seven thirty and we still needed to shop for groceries. I suggested we get his pants another time. It was not at all like this son of mine to put up a fuss. But that night he did. "You always do this," John accused. I mustered up the energy to keep going. Much relieved when we quickly found new dress pants for him at Biltmore Shopping Center. Finally, at our last stop—Smitty's grocery. John asked to make a special dessert for all of us. He had in mind a cantaloupe bowl, complete with fruit and ice cream. I let him pick out what he wanted.

Chapter 24

The house was dark when we drove up shortly before nine. I felt an immediate tinge of disappointment, wished Roger and the kids were back already. Seemed they should have been home by now. I put the groceries away, while John got busy making five desserts.

Half an hour passed. It was out of character for Roger to keep the little ones out this late. He ought to have called. John decided he didn't want to wait any longer and polished off his dessert while watching TV. Past ten my annoyance turned to concern. "Mom, Don't worry," was John's quick response. "They'll be here soon." Shortly after ten thirty, my son went to bed. I didn't say anything more about their absence. No need to worry him if he wasn't worried. I was already doing enough of that for both of us. My husband and I often discussed the possibility of an accident. Though in Roger's mind there was no such possibility. At least none that he would admit to. "It is safer to fly than to drive." He'd used that line on me countless times. Always he reminded me that he could glide the plane down in case of a mechanical emergency. Highways and open spaces were everywhere. I shouldn't worry.

No longer could I quiet my mind. They were now very late. I conjured up all kinds of mindscapes. They had landed safely in the desert. There was mechanical failure. They were waiting for daylight. Roger would call as soon as he could get to a phone. They would be here in the morning. All other scenarios were red hot. It took my breath away to think that way. I dared not finish the thought. When midnight came, there was no longer any doubt they were down. Roger would have called if he could. My brain was sizzling, my emotions churning. I couldn't help them. I didn't even know where to look. I didn't know what to do. My mind was not allowing me solutions. Was Kenny dropped off? It was as if I was paralyzed by fear. I prayed constantly. Prayed on my knees for their safety and for their lives. I couldn't bear to think of them irreparably maimed and in pain. And the unthinkable—how could we ever live without them? I pleaded for their safe return.

It was almost two in the morning. I felt as though I was going to jump right out of my skin. I hauled out my vacuum. Methodically, I vacuumed every inch of the house except John's bedroom. John would know soon enough. The droning noise of the vacuum had a calming effect. But not nearly enough to drown out my desperation or keep at bay the searing pain churning deep within my gut. *Maybe this could just be a very bad dream?* I was getting so tired. *I mustn't give in to that. Roger will call and tell me they are okay. He'll want me to know they are safe. I need to stay awake and wait for his call.*

I finished vacuuming. I was just going to get off my feet for a bit. Still fully dressed, I dozed off. When I awoke with a start, I had been asleep for almost two hours. My bedside light was on. Roger's side of the bed was undisturbed. There was no escaping this. All around me loomed a dark and bitter hollowness, a huge and ominous void. This was not a dream. My throat was constricting. It was hard to swallow. It was hard to breathe. Nothing seemed real anymore. When morning light dawned in the east, I finally called the tower at Scottsdale airport. The person who answered could not help me. There was no flight plan filed for the plane. Then, I remembered. My husband had issues with this control tower in the past. Back in March I'd received an emergency call from the tower to let me know his plane was late. It was the end of spring break, and Roger and our boys and my sister were skiing in Utah. That call from the tower had caused a frantic twenty minutes of distress, then Roger walked in with the kids in tow. He'd wanted me to come along on that skiing trip. Had begged me. But I'd had this pressing feeling that I should stay home with the little ones. And my parents were still visiting.

In a daze I dialed the home of our second counselor in the bishopric. I heard myself say impossible words. This was real.

Almost immediately our home filled with friends and neighbors. Others took over. It was comforting to no longer be alone with this. Private planes went up to search the flight path from Phoenix to

Page. News traveled fast. I was getting phone calls from near and far, even from concerned strangers. Silent prayers were offered on behalf of my family. I was both numb and gripped by the pain of fear. But there was also a palpable feeling of being carried, a feeling of being enveloped in a loving and protective, soft cocoon.

John was in denial. "Why are all these people here?" His hand gripped my shoulder, and he whispered into my ear, "They'll be back, Mom." Then he went away with his friend Tim. Late afternoon Tim's family took John out for dinner. These good neighbors were the first to arrive at our home that early morning, even before seven.

Eventually, I went to lie down in my bedroom. There was no longer any way to justify Roger's absence. Paralyzing fear permanently settled in my bones. Information reached us that a plane's distress signal was intercepted. I recognized the mountainous area on a map. We'd flown over many times. For a while our Relief Society president was with me. Anne gently stroked my back. I wished for sleep. But fear and impossible thoughts fired up my brain. Anne came in again. The plane had been located and positively identified. Our stake president, followed by three elders, entered our courtyard. I watched them, each with his head bowed, file past the large living room window under the portico. And I knew what I was about to hear.

I do not recall who bid them inside. Somehow, I stood on the raised Saltillo tile entry surrounded by these four men, who, only hours earlier, flew over the site of the plane crash. I was numb. I do not recall what was said. My only real memory of these desperately tragic moments is the sudden feeling of weakness seeping into my knees. As if my knees were slowly filling with Jell-O. At the same time a strange sensation crept along my spine. Then it hit me—I was about to collapse.

The very instant this realization hit, I determined that this must not happen. No way was my twelve-year old-son coming home to find his mother incapacitated—only to have it confirmed that his father and his younger brother and sister were gone from our lives. I could not let that happen. Unseen hands were surely there to hold me up, to steady me and to strengthen me. I could not have continued standing on my own power with such undermining weakness seeping into my knees and creeping along my spine.

President Shumway alerted several of our closest neighbors. Sometime later, Dick and Lorraine walked over from across the street. Dick took me firmly into his arms. He wouldn't let go. For the longest time he just held me tight. We cried together. I didn't know how we could go on. How could we live without them? My kind neighbor's firm and loving embrace was a soothing balm to my shattered soul. It was only a few days ago that Roger and Dick spent more than an hour in conversation on our front lawn. Nothing seemed real anymore. This loving couple never stopped caring. Dick and Loraine were in their late forties. They had no children. Whenever Dick considered making improvements to their home, he'd come over and ask what I thought about it. Then he handled all arrangements. I will always remember the true Christian love and kindness offered us by this thoughtful couple, who so regularly ministered to us. And that wasn't all. Neighbors, friends, and our ward family reached out to us. Their love was palpable. All were ministering angels. Their support and love was so invaluable during this most difficult time.

When John arrived home, I sensed it was dawning on him what he was about to hear. I took him into the privacy of my bedroom. My heart was so heavy. I cradled my young son's face in my hands and spoke to him words no child should have to hear. "Daddy and Leslie and Jeddie have gone to live with our Father in heaven."

My son stared at me with an incredulous expression of disbelief in his wide-open eyes. "You mean... they died?" Desperately, he sobbed in my arms. We cried together. After a while John composed himself. "But, Mom, I was so mean to them." I was flabbergasted to hear his self-recrimination. Leslie and Jeddie adored him. Those three always had so much fun together. Almost daily, when he came home from school, John would wrestle with Jedd. His little brother waited for this playtime. Perhaps John was a little rough on occasion, like older brothers can be. "Jeddie was so tough, Mom. He was such a cool little brother." John sobbed again. We sat on my bed and shared memories. More recently John had persuaded Leslie to make peanut butter sandwiches for his school lunches. I gave my boys lunch money at the start of each week. If they wanted to bring lunch from home, they were allowed to keep the money saved. But they had to prepare their own lunch. John had paid Leslie a quarter to make his sandwich. That made her happy! And there was still money left over for him to keep. I assured John that he was a wonderful big brother, for he truly was. His siblings adored him.

My heart felt shredded. My young son would have to grow up without his father to guide him. Pensively, John confided, "I've been waiting to be old enough for Dad to teach me things. Now, he's not going to be able to do that." Disbelief and confusion mingled with physical pain. Pain, for our broken lives, for myself, for my young son, and for his three older siblings, who still needed to be told. At the same time, I was undeniably imbued by a strengthening peace. It was a feeling of peace that overwhelmingly surpassed my understanding. How was this even possible? We'd lost so much. Throughout this most difficult day, I had rested my soul in this strange phenomenon and silently pondered the juxtaposition.

Over and over in my mind scrolled Proverbs 3:5–6. "Trust in the Lord with all thine heart, and lean not unto thine own understanding. In all thy ways acknowledge him, and he shall direct thy paths." Prayerfully, I clung to my faith. It was all I had left.

It seemed ironic that lifesaving instructions were posted inside our kitchen and bathroom cabinets. Emergency phone numbers. CPR instruction! Poison control. It was posted in every home we ever lived in. I made sure of that. Yet I couldn't save my family.

The plane crash was located on the north side of Humphrey's Peak in the San Francisco Mountains in Flagstaff. On Thursday evening around seven twenty-five, the very time that John and I had been shopping, a couple observed a sudden flash of bright light followed immediately by a plume of thick, black smoke that came billowing up from the mountain. They hadn't known what it was, until they saw on the news that a plane was missing. Friends picked Stacy up at the airport and brought her home. She had received the tragic news from her uncle in Laguna Beach. I was grateful for her resolute and strong attitude. Only weeks from turning twenty-four, she'd now lost both biological parents. Growing up, Stacy was my right hand. Devoted to her brothers, she was a great help at home. Her siblings adored her. That first long night, Stacy, John, and I huddled in my bedroom. We'd settled on a musical number for the service of our loved ones, "You'll Never Walk Alone," by Rogers and Hammerstein. Like tiny seedlings of hope sprouting from a barren desert, the music accompanying those strengthening lyrics came floating through my head while we talked.

Our house was eerily quiet when I opened my eyes early Saturday morning. No familiar sounds were coming from my children's bedrooms. No little feet came running down the hall. My babies didn't come bouncing onto my bed. They didn't need me anymore. Never again would they need me. Never again would my husband sleep by my side. I felt strangely vulnerable and exposed. It was like I was no longer me. My lower arms seemed detached from my body. Who was I? Somehow I had to find courage to face this new day. Courage to face a whole new life. I hadn't wanted a new life. I wasn't given a choice. Soothing water from my hot shower mingled with cascades of salty tears springing from my eyes. Down the drain they went. Like my life. I could no longer will my tears to stop. On this eerily quiet Saturday morning in early June, I was unaware that I had yet to be introduced to the nearly unbearable pain of grieving. Brought home in the private plane of friends in our ward, Ken arrived at the Executive Terminal at Phoenix Sky Harbor early Saturday afternoon. Seared into my memory is my distraught fifteen-year-old as he stepped through the open door of the plane. Deeply shaken, my sorrowing teenage son descended the stairs and fell into my arms. "Oh, Mom, had I only known, I wouldn't have asked Dad to fly me to Lake Powell."

It was Roger's idea to fly our son to Lake Powell. Knowing that a positive spiritual element was part of summer camp, we wanted him to have this experience with the youth and adult leaders from our ward. When, due to a prior commitment Ken couldn't leave with the group, his father offered to fly him up. It was an easy jaunt from Scottsdale to Page and back.

It took decades for Ken to come to terms with this tragic accident. That it was not his fault. Though, I have had regrets that I opted out on this trip. I've never felt to blame myself for sending my children with their father. Accidents happen. It is easy to become convinced that one's presence might have changed the outcome. Many months after the accident, John confided, "If only I had not been chicken. They might not have died." He was just a young boy of twelve. Survivor's guilt is real. For more than a year before the life-changing summer of 1982, I had unusual premonitions. They were unsettling. Some cannot be shared. Very deliberately I pushed them aside. Now, however, with our loved ones gone from our earthly existence, it seemed to me that the final pieces to an unusual puzzle had at last been discovered and put into place.

A favorite photo of our two youngest children was on display in our living room. A full year before the accident, as I held that lovely gold-framed eight-by-ten in my hands, I received this disturbing impression: *One day you'll hold this picture and they will not be here.*

I was stunned, had fled the room in tears. It was impossible for me to want believe such a terrible thing. I wondered why crazy thoughts like that would even enter my mind. Now, in my deepest distress, my mind turned to my patriarchal blessing. I was given this special inspired blessing exactly one week before my twenty-first birthday. All that day I had fasted and prayed in preparation for the evening meeting with our stake patriarch, who had declared an unsettling statement while pronouncing the blessing. A week later, a typewritten copy arrived in our mailbox. At the end of the second paragraph, it did indeed state, "You will have a sweetness in motherhood, even though there will be anguish connected therewith."

The word *anguish* had immediately stung. It was difficult to concentrate on the remainder of the blessing, because *anguish* was bouncing up and down in my brain. I hoped it didn't mean what I thought it meant. At home I consulted my dictionary. There was no escaping that ominous word—*anguish*.

I decided not to think about it. Intruding thoughts were pushed aside. Perhaps this word was alluding to my raising stepchildren. And that is what I told myself. There were many sweet and tender moments when raising Mark and Stacy. But it was often a challenge. Now, in my deepest despair, it was given me to understand that I had in fact been blessed with foreknowledge. That sentence in my patriarchal blessing, that for years caused such consternation, became a true comfort as I endeavored to come to terms with the immense tragedy that so suddenly had interrupted our lives. Through my faith in the atonement of my elder brother, Jesus Christ, I was given the ability to accept the passing of my loved ones. I couldn't fathom how we would go on without my husband and my beautiful little children. I knew only this one thing—I could not let my faith falter.

On a particularly difficult day, I came across a quote by Franklin D. Roosevelt: "When you get to the end of your rope, tie a knot in it and hang on." I had tied that knot long ago. Tied it firmly to my faith in God. During my darkest days, when it felt that my life was dangling dangerously over a deep precipice, it was a helpful image to think of standing on that firmly tied knot.

"Phoenix doesn't seem like home anymore without Dad here." It was the first Sunday without them. Mark's plane had arrived from Salt Lake City. He was right. Nothing was the same.

A friend stopped by the house with a booklet written by President Spencer W. Kimball. His words in *Tragedy or Destiny* resonated strongly with me. "In the face of apparent tragedy, we must put our trust in God, knowing that despite our limited view His purposes will not fail." *What could be God's purpose for this terrible tragedy?* I couldn't begin to fathom. Yet my heart was steadily given peace. Somehow, it was given me to be able to accept that God's purpose will be revealed to me when my earthly existence is fulfilled. My final hours spent with my beloved family members played frequently on my mind. *What if I had not agreed to pick up my children from the sitter's house?* Inexplicably, those words, that initially took form in my conscience, were never spoken to my husband. It was as if they were lifted right off my tongue and substituted by kinder, more thoughtful words. I shuttered to think how very close I came to forfeiting the final sweet moments with my precious babies. All for the sake of a nap! Mercifully, I was shielded from a lifetime of regrets.

The more I thought about my husband and our little children laid to rest in three separate caskets, the more unthinkable this became. I needed to know that my babies were resting in their father's arms. Only this was conceivable. Roger would have wanted that. On Thursday, June 10, one week after our loved ones left us, we arrived for the funeral. Ahead of the service, we joined family and close friends in the Relief Society room for a private meeting. Ken had early on expressed his desire to be one of the speakers. His siblings followed suit. John would be first. My twelve-year-old had been so quietly stoic through-out the past devastating week. As we approached the meeting house, he began to weep. No longer was John sure he could walk up to the podium and face the mourners. I assured him he didn't have to. As the lone casket was wheeled slowly into the chapel, our arms linked together, and the five of us faced the crowd of mourners who completely filled the chapel and the large cultural hall. Methodically, we made our way to the second front row of the middle pew in the chapel. This is where Roger and I had been seated with our children on most Sundays for the past six years. The choir loft behind the podium was com-pletely filled with beautiful floral arrangements. The casket was centered below the podium directly in front of us. Cascading over the top of the casket was a large arrangement of eighteen red roses amid a sea of white carnations. Because I loved white carnations, my husband had always brought me a lovely bouquet for our anniversary. For each year of our marriage, Roger had added a red rose. Less than a month had passed since we celebrated our eighteenth anniversary. In the twinkling of an eye, our years together had come to an abrupt halt.

As the opening hymn came to a close, I watched my twelve-year-old son straighten his back and wipe away his tears. "I'm going to do it," he whispered to me. Following the invocation, John walked resolutely to the podium, where he confidently addressed the immense crowd before him. In his young, tender voice, John related some of his experiences with his younger sister and brother and shared how his father would go out of his way to do things for each of us. Ken spoke of his last moments with his father and his two younger siblings. He had lifted his little brother into his arms and hugged and kissed him, told Jeddie he loved him. He and Leslie had hugged. He had bent down and kissed her cheek. And he'd told his sister that he loved her. He'd hugged and kissed his father, something he hadn't done in a long while. "I thanked him for taking me. He said he was glad to do it." About forty minutes after parting, Ken heard the loud noise of a plane flying over the campsite. "There was my dad flying over camp, waggling the wings like he'd done so many times before." My husband had regularly announced his homecoming by flying directly over our home upon his return to Scottsdale Airpark.

Stacy expressed her gratitude for the time she was able to spend with her father and her younger sister and brother. "Leslie and Jedd taught us all something. They were so outgoing and so loving. We were lucky we had them and had such a wonderful father," she said.

Mark shared about his relationship with his father. Then he added, "I came home trying to comfort the family and ended up being comforted. My mother has been a strength to all of us." Later, he confided to me in private, "When we buried my father is when I buried my mother." The family had thought it best to spare Mark and Stacy the sadness of their mother's funeral service. This had unfortunately proven to be to Mark's detriment.

My brother-in-law, Chris, as well as Stake President Shumway were the final speakers. The immense outpouring of love and compassion was palpable. We felt protected and carried by this wave of love and prayers flowing so abundantly into our lives from family, friends, neighbors, and even many strangers and angels unseen. This comforting and soothing feeling of sustaining love had literally held us up during the many difficult days of the past week.

The hearse was waiting curbside in front of the church. Pensively my children and I seated ourselves in the black limousine parked behind. I was still holding the program and pondered the first line of the brief poem printed on front: *We give our loved ones back to God.* I hadn't wanted to give them back. It was never a choice.

As the hearse slowly rolled off the church parking lot, our limo followed close behind. Visible through the back window was the lone casket holding my forty-six-year-old husband, my steadfast and loving companion of eighteen years. The father of my children! In his arms lay my youngest son and daughter. How was this even real?

In the solemn quietness of the back seat, a truth silently claimed its way into my battered consciousness. Softly I shared my thought, "This is not the end. This is a new beginning."

Without warning, John folded himself into my lap. Deep, mournful sobs rose from the chambers of my twelve-year-old son's shattered heart. His slim boyish back shook under his crisp white cotton shirt. My own heart was already bleeding profusely. The funeral possession continued its way to Paradise Memorial Gardens on Shea Boulevard in Scottsdale. Police escorts roared alongside.

For the five of us, the fragility of life was on full display. We'd driven this route countless times, when life was real and our days still normal. On this Thursday afternoon, everything around us seemed foreign and unfamiliar. Only two weeks earlier, we had driven to Lake Saguaro along this route. On that pleasant family day we had no way of knowing that this was the beginning of the end. Roger had brought me a sunflower in the form of a plastic windmill—a flower that could never die. Only from hindsight can we see clearly into the future.

Because my husband loved the water, I chose two cemetery plots along water's edge. On that long, hot day in early June, my own demise could not come soon enough. At the graveside service, I functioned mechanically, as if outside myself. Vaguely, I remember being handed a triangular folded flag at the end of the Veteran's ceremony. My mind has retained no other memory of this ceremony.

A generous buffet was served in our home by Relief Society sisters. A friend was at the piano playing her music softly. The penetrating fragrance from white lilies filled our home. Their pungent smell was getting to me. Apparently, I'd brushed too close against some of these elegant white petals. A broad streak of yellow dust marked the side of my pale-lilac skirt. Never again would I choose to wear this lovely two-piece silk dress. I'd found it while shopping with my sister-in-law. As usual, when together, Liz and I joked and laughed. All the while I'd wondered, *How is it possible to still laugh when all joy has left my soul?* That afternoon a flash reminder, that soon would no longer be familiar, had guiltily crept into my mind. *You've been gone too long, you need to get home to your little children!* Almost immediately the stark new reality of my life penetrated my pained consciousness. *They don't need me anymore.*

Chapter 25

Was there anything in my life that made me deserving of this unthinkable loss? In the quietness of many dark nights, I scanned my memory and posed this question to myself and to my God. My answer came with *peace*, that peace that surpasses all understanding. A friend shared with me that my young daughter was found outside the plane, resting across her father's chest. For weeks I agonized over desperate images conjured up by my imagination. *Was my little girl alive after the crash? Did Leslie make her way outside to her father's body? Was she trying to find comfort in her daddy's lifeless arms? Or was Roger overcome, as he lay mortally injured, yet bravely attempted to carry Leslie to safety?* Impossible thoughts were killing me. Enlightenment came weeks after they were gone.

"Whatever happened, when the plane went down, is over." Yes, it was over. Silently as I sang into the night "Abide With Me, Tis Eventide," it stopped the wild racing of my heart.

It was my first day back to work. I'd been off for several weeks. Systematically, I'd worked through my hourly patients. An escalating pressure came on suddenly at the end of day.

Doc had invited our staff to lunch, as he did almost weekly. When the server came for our drink order, I boldly requested Scotch on the rocks. That broke the ice. As the laughter dampened, I changed my order to Coca-Cola. All morning the staff had tiptoed around me. It was difficult to be the odd woman out. These days it felt like that most of the time. I was a widow. I was a mother without her precious babies. Frankly, I wasn't at all sure who or what I was anymore. Mostly, it seemed I was walking alone in a vast, empty desert. Walking in uncharted territory! This empty feeling came from inside of me. Because everything was so different. But it came from outside as well. No one was guilty. It was just the way it was. I'd done it myself, watched someone who was bereaved with sad eyes. Or purposely not made eye contact. Turned away, not knowing what to say. It was as if I belonged to an isolated species of homo sapiens. In truth, more often than not, there were words of sincere condolence. Warm, caring hugs. Gifts. Flowers. Cards. Phone calls. Invitations! Friends reaching out with love and kindness. This loving support was so instrumental to our ability to cope and move forward, so absolutely necessary for our survival and our healing. I learned for myself that words are not necessary. Spirit speaks to spirit without words.

The pressure started building the minute I escorted my last patient to the front desk. In no time this pressure grew to the intensity of having to vomit. Even stronger than that. I felt a deep need to vomit

out everything inside me. I made it out of the parking lot and purposely steered the car in the opposite direction from home. Then came the screams!
Horrific sounds were coming from the very depth of
my soul. Raw and piercing, these screams were shock-
ing in their intensity. It seemed there were two of me.
Incredulously, one of me was doing this unthinkable screaming. Finally, the screams lost intensity.
Sobbing, I could barely see to drive. *No one must* ever
hear this. They'll think I've lost my mind. Instinctively
I knew I hadn't. The sudden attack had released the
intense pressure that without warning welled up
within me. Left was a well-known and painful void
that seemed, these days, to ever be with me.

Our house came into view seconds after I
steered Roger's car onto our street. I pressed the automatic garage door opener. The contents that used
to be stored inside were systematically exposed. In
my mind's eye, I saw it all, the bright orange-col-
ored Little Tikes Coupe, Leslie's cherished pink bike
parked right next to it. She had so recently learned
to ride without help or training wheels. Memories
and pictures erupted in my brain as I pulled forward
into the garage. I wanted them home. I wanted my
family back. I felt weak and trapped in my yearning
for what used to be.

Both my boys were there. My mother had dinner almost ready. I hurried directly into what had
absurdly become my own bedroom. I changed into
my robe, spent a few minutes in what was now my
very own bathroom. I needed to wash my face and

repair the damage. *What in the world happened to my life?* Everything seemed so meaningless.

Calmly I joined my family at the dinner table. Had I just washed off this whole crazy episode? One month had passed since the accident. Seemed life had returned to normal for most people. It was not so at our place. Like a rogue ocean wave, grief pain came crashing without warning, knocked me about and sent me to my knees. It was often as if every cell and fiber in my body were being crushed. I wasn't always home, where I could find refuge in the corner of my bathroom and curl into fetal position.

It was easy to want to wallow in misery. One day I opted to stay in bed. *Why fight it?* By two o'clock in the afternoon, I couldn't do it anymore. It proved unbearably more miserable to wallow. I prayed for strength and the ability to endure.

I gave thoughts to suicide. Yet it was never about suicide. It was self-indulgent thinking. Taking my own life would solve nothing. I could never have chosen to add to my children's sorrow. Basically, I was allowing myself to think of ways to escape this monstrous pain. Deep down I realized this kind of thinking was not realistic. Nor was it wise. There was going to be pain for a long while. I *had* to find hope. It was innate. By far my better option. I prayed for strength to endure to the end. And I studied my scriptures. Somehow, this always brought me peace.

I soon came to realize that my thoughts had immense power. How I thought about life was a strong indicator of how my day went. Every thought mattered. Every thought directed how I felt. When I focused my thoughts on our loss, I went down fast. It was always helpful to count my blessings. Gratitude focused my thoughts on the positives in my life.

Before my parents were scheduled to fly home to Denmark, my mother found me lying prone on the floor in my bedroom. Somehow this position was comforting. Not that I could even try to explain why. My father sat me down for a heart-to-heart talk. "Keep your faith," he said. "Don't allow this difficult loss to embitter your heart and your life or the lives of your remaining children." He suggested that I had many years left and added, "Don't let this tragedy rob you of your youth or your vitality!" I knew he was right. My father was always my hero. He was still convalescing from prostate surgery performed only days before the accident. I had been sure his surgery would prevent them from traveling. How grateful I was when he assured me, "Don't worry about me. We're going to be with you through this."

Chapter 26

Two months had passed since our loved ones so abruptly left us. It was impossible for me to accept that I had not gotten to say goodbye. I could not let it go. I wanted so much to hold them, just one more time.

One night I had a dream. I felt tugging on my skirt without being conscious of his presence, until I heard my youngest son calling to me, "Mommy, Mommy." Then instantly, Jeddie was in my arms. I pressed my precious little boy close against me. His skinny little arms wrapped tightly around my neck. From the bottom of my feet I felt my body fill with the power of healing. The emptiness inside me filled the same way one fills a bottle. Throughout those treasured moments, I was perfectly aware that I would need to let him go again. His presence was a gift. Jeddie was not mine to keep. *Oh, God*, my heart cried out. *If only I can have this kind of experience now and then, I can survive this.*

For a short while I was alone again. Then, I caught sight of Leslie. She was standing on the opposite side of a wide rectangular pool. Diamonds shimmered in bright sunlight on crystal-blue water. Leslie's long blond hair was disheveled, as if she'd just gotten out of bed. I watched her rubbing her eyes with both hands. When she looked up, her eyes widened in pure delight. "Mommy! Oh, Mommy!" Leslie's voice sounded as joyful as my heart felt. Clearly, she was as surprised to see me as I was to see her. Her arms stretched out toward me, and instantly Leslie was in my arms. Oh, to feel her solid body. As I held my precious daughter tight, I savored that familiar feeling of my little girl's legs wrapped around my waist. I pressed her close against my heart. My little girl's arms were wrapped tightly around my neck.

It was almost two in the morning when I opened my eyes. My heart brimmed to overflowing with joy. I had held their solid bodies. Had indeed felt my beloved children's loving embrace. The feel of their bodies still so vividly with me. I saw my husband. But he didn't come close. I felt he'd brought my children to me. They were so young. Surely, they still needed their mother. Though I was without my companion, it was somehow comforting for me to know that their father was with them. My heart felt immense gratitude for this amazing experience. Since that long-ago night, there has sparingly been additional experiences with my angel children. Each has been a source of deepest healing to my wounded soul.

Friends would ask, "How do you do it?" Obviously not without difficulty! And never on my own power. Unquestionably, I am given daily strength through the grace and power of the atonement of Jesus Christ. Deep within my soul is the undeniable awareness that Christ is with me through this. He has helped carry the burden of this immense loss. And this we are promised in the scriptures.

A healing peace attends me more often than not. Through the atonement of Jesus Christ, I have been given help to accept the passing of my loved ones. Gratefully, I have been spared from harboring bitterness and anger at God. Mercifully, I have been spared regrets. During those final days with my loved ones, I was clearly guided to alter my intentions. Christ is aware of me. He is aware of each and every one of us. He will walk with us though our deepest sorrows. And he will carry us when we can't go on. He knows and has personally experienced all our individual pain and our sorrows.

I have gained a heightened awareness of all that I have to be grateful for. I am eternally grateful for my family and for many special friends who lovingly and generously held me up. They are our earthly angels who love us and stay close in happy times as well as in difficult times. I am gratefully aware that heavenly angels attend us as well.

But we missed them each and every single day. As a single parent, my hands were full. We were all hurting and struggling with our new reality. It often seemed a heavy anchor was tied firmly to our lives. Our loss intruded into every thought and every deed. First and foremost, I wanted my children to know that it was possible to once again find joy and happiness.

Though I never saw his face, I have felt Christ walking with me as if we were shoulder to shoulder. I shared my testimony with my mother-in-law, Lola, in Laguna Beach. She too lost a child. Lost her son and two grandchildren. In her suffering, her faith was sometimes wavering. I wrote her a letter. A portion is included below.

> On my last birthday, Roger gave me *The Living Bible*. It was really for himself, he'd told me, for he enjoyed reading the Bible in this paraphrased version. A few weeks ago, I turned to the chapter of Job in this Bible. Under the heading Theme is written: "The mystery that surrounds human existence and the need to trust in God runs throughout the book. Mankind simply does not have enough knowledge to explain why things happen the way they do. It is possible to rise above our limitations by faith in God, however, because God does know why things happen and will work good for those who love him. *We may thus learn the profound truth that when we have nothing left but God, God is enough.*"

Firsts were difficult, our emotions still so raw. Yet there was much good in our days. My boys and I traveled to Laguna Beach regularly. It was comforting to walk around this lovely beach town, where many wonderful memories were made during the years my children were growing up. It was comforting to be with extended family.

We created new memories even as we cherished the old. The boys and I continued our family tradition of waterskiing trips to Lake Saguaro. We always invited friends to join us. I learned to put the boat in the water. A feeling of empowerment strengthened me as I learned to do many things on my own.

Often, we stumbled in our pain. Much we kept hidden within ourselves, as if to shield each other from further anguish. Ours was the difficult task to not allow our loss to define us. John broke down one afternoon after I picked him up from a friend's house. He'd been introduced to another family as "the boy whose father and sister and brother died in a plane crash." Through bitter tears, my young son protested, "That is not who I am, Mom." Kenny lamented his need for his father's guiding influence. He had decisions to make regarding college and his future. "I love you, Mom, but it's not enough."

Of course it wasn't enough. My sons so desperately needed the influence of a strong male role model. Both my boys shared with me that they felt embarrassed by the plane crash. They'd expected their father to be invincible. It was humbling for them to learn that he was not. Stacy visited regularly from California. My sister came to live with us until she married in late fall of '83. Eventually, Mark came home from BYU and stayed with us until he married in the spring of '83. We learned to function as a different family unit. And we tried extra hard to look for the good in our lives. Though, one night, John cryptically asked, "What family, Mom?"

Once again I rounded the top of the hill and flew past the fast-food restaurant in Page where I'd dropped off my boys. I was trying to decide if I should follow my sudden urge to drive to the airport? I had about half an hour to myself before we again hit the road.

It was spring break. My boys and I were caravanning to Brian Head along with several families from our ward. Our journey from Phoenix had started out in high spirits. We looked forward to three full days of skiing and fun. When the snow-covered San Francisco Peaks came into view, a quiet pensiveness settled over the three of us. As the curve of the freeway took us around the mountains in Flagstaff, Ken pointed left. "Mom, it's over there." A friend had flown him to Flagstaff only days after the accident. They'd hiked part of the way up the mountain to the crash site. Abandoned on the rugged tree-covered hillside lay one of Leslie's new red leather sandals. Two silver gum wrappers were nearby. Ken had given each of his siblings a stick of gum during the flight. The plane was brand-new when Roger and two partners purchased the turbo-charged single engine white and brown Cessna 210 in 1980. Somehow, I never learned to feel comfortable with this purchase.

I parked by the airport. I needed to retrace the final steps my husband and my two babies walked on earth. We'd always first made a beeline for the restrooms. I pictured my children running ahead of their father, excited and laughing, as they made their way inside the terminal before takeoff. It was still so easy to become lost in memories of untouchable yesterdays. Twenty-one months had passed since that fateful night and still unexpected emotional stumbling blocks surfaced. It had not been my plan to stop by this small airport in Page. I hadn't planned to spend this time reliving the past. This was supposed to be a fun trip. Instead, it affected me like my first trip to the grocery store after Roger and the kids were gone. As I walked the aisles alone, I came to realize that the need to purchase many of the usual grocery items was gone. I had rushed home empty-handed. Lost myself. Without my little children by my side, it felt as if my arms were amputated below the elbows. For most of my adult life, my two hands were linked to two trusting smaller hands.

On my mind played Jeddie's pensive attitude the day he and I went to Olan Mills to have his picture taken. He'd seemed so far away in his thoughts, so unusually pensive for my little man. *Had angels that day whispered to him secrets of a journey he was about to take? Were they secrets he wasn't allowed to share with his mommy?* The day after he and his sister were laid to rest in their father's arms was the day the studio had called to let me know the pictures of my son were ready to be picked up. When I again stepped outside the Page terminal to drive back to pick up my teenage sons, it was as if God himself cupped his hands around my aching heart and whispered into my ear, "I know how much this hurts...and I am so sorry."

"Mom, life is really not that different now. It's just...they never come back." John was sweeping the garage. I was grateful for his comment. I was trying hard to keep whatever normalcy was possible. We grew ever stronger as we engaged in new activities. Regularly, we climbed Squaw Peak. Symbolically, I searched the clouds for silver linings. Up high, next to the benchmark, I imagined conquering my emotional mountain. I'd memorized the lyrics to Rogers and Hammerstein's "You'll Never Walk Alone." The master healer was ever with me.

The boys stayed busy with school and sports. They ran marathons. When they crossed the finish line, I was there waiting for them. As always, I cheered them on during football games, basketball games, and track meets. When a friend challenged me to train for a 10K, we ran the Crescent City Run in New Orleans together. I finished a real estate course and obtained my license, something Roger had encouraged me to do for years. Mark asked what I wanted my grandchildren to call me. Since Grandpa wasn't around, I opted for Omie. That's German for grandma! This started a new fun chapter in our lives. It was wonderful to have my married sister living in close proximity. Sisterhood was a whole new and gratifying chapter in our lives. Stacy visited regularly from California. A beautiful young woman, she had several marriage prospects. Upon graduating BYU, Stacy accepted a five-month student-teaching assignment in South Wales. Slowly and surely, we each went about rebuilding our lives. At different times each of my children came to me and suggested I was too young to stay single. Even my mother-in-law broached the subject. "Karin, I pray every day that you'll find a good man to marry."

Robin and I met on the last day of June in 1986. As usual, I lay awake quite early that Monday morning. Eventually, I hauled out my bike and was soon riding around the Biltmore Circle. Beautiful older estates on large lots surround the green manicured golf course in this prestigious Phoenix neighborhood. The elegant historic 1929 Arizona Biltmore Resort is focal point. I pedaled fast around the circle several times. At last I turned up a short hill toward the Arizona Canal, where a dirt trail stretches along the canal banks in both directions.

I immediately noticed the bearded guy coming from my left just as I pedaled up to the trail. He had a huge smile on his face. Not in the mood to be social so early in the morning, I pedaled my bike faster for distance. He kept up. Stayed right behind me when I turned down Thirty-Second Street toward my new home. I had moved into a two-bedroom, two-bath apartment at Del Prado only the week before. Ken was at ASU. John and I didn't need a big house anymore, and I'd felt the need for a change. When I jumped off my bike in front of the guard house, I heard a pleasant voice behind me, "Don't tell me you live here too." So he hadn't been following me. That humbled me a little. We walked our bikes almost side by side when I decided to introduce myself. His name was Robin Ford. He seemed pleasant enough.

The next day I came home from work to find a sticky note on my apartment door. The note was an invitation from Robin to join him for an early morning bike ride on July 4, followed by breakfast at a nearby restaurant. He was clearly resourceful. I hadn't given him my apartment number during our brief introduction. Robin had left two phone numbers. I waited till the next day to call him at his office. His secretary answered the phone, "Maricopa County Psychological Services!" I had guessed he was a mental health specialist. The bottom of his sticky note was imprinted with *Charter Hospital by the Sea.* That gave me a clue. His beard kinda gave him away. Over breakfast I learned that Robin was new in town. He'd chosen to come to Phoenix when recruited by Maricopa County Sheriff's Office. As clinical psychologist, he was responsible for conduct-ing preemployment evaluations for law enforcement and detention officers. And his department offered counseling services for their employees.

Robin had moved to Phoenix from Georgia, had lived at Del Prado for all but three weeks. A twice-divorced father of three sons and a daughter, he grew up in Rockford, Illinois, as an only child. Adopted from infancy, he was brought up in his par-

ents' Catholic faith. His folks still lived in his childhood home on Harvard Avenue. From first grade
through college, he'd attended Catholic schools. My
new friend had obtained his doctorate in psychology from Northern Illinois University, though, an
unfortunate chain of events preceded this. Having
obtained his master's in clinical psychology in 1965
from the University of Rochester in New York, he
wished to immediately continue his studies at the
University of Chicago. By spring of 1968, Robin had
enough credits to complete his doctorate. Needing
financial assistance to afford this, he submitted his
application for a scholarship. At this same time, the
Students for a Democratic Society took over the U
of C's administration building. Having dug a trench
around the administration building, they prevented
access to school records. Led by Bernie Sanders, these
student radicals trashed the offices and scattered on
the floor, room after room, the contents of filing cabinets. Because this included all scholarship applications submitted that spring, no scholarships would
be available.

Robin chose to finish his studies at Northern
Illinois University at DeKalb. Paying for his studies out of pocket, he was able to complete his doctorate and dissertation within a year and a half. In
adulthood, Robin embraced several religions such as
Unitarian, Presbyterian, Lutheran, Methodist, and
Quaker. He revealed this religious smorgasbord on
our first date after inquiring if I attended church.
Because our conversation continued in this vein, I

invited him to join us on Sunday. Though it was my custom to share my faith with new acquaintances, I did not expect him to accept my invitation. Nor had I intended to invite him. At least not that day! There was an honest intelligence about him. I liked his clear blue eyes. But I didn't yet know the man. Inviting Robin to join us, however, seemed the only proper thing to do, based on our conversation.

In the back of my mind was also Robin's thoughtful response to my sixteen-year-old son that morning. Dressed to go out, we were leaving my apartment. They'd only just met, when John voiced concern about an unusual sound in the used car, a sky-blue Bronco II purchased only days earlier. Yet Robin suggested, "Let's go take a look, John," and immediately led the way to the parking lot with my son trailing behind. As I followed them, my thoughts were that I should take a closer look at this man. During breakfast, it became clear that Robin and I were destined to meet. His Georgia dentist had advised him that there was only one dentist in Phoenix he should go to! By pure chance, this was the same dentist recommended to my family when we came to Phoenix from Santa Barbara in 1967. When Robin and I met, I worked as a dental hygienist in this very office.

Five months and three days after we met, we were married in Odense, Denmark. My youngest brother, Carsten, who served as bishop in Odense Ward, performed the wedding. Six months after our marriage, Robin made the choice to be baptized. Before we met, he knew nothing about our church. He remembered, however, that he had watched a 1976 bicentennial program on TV with his young family while he still lived in Illinois. The Mormon trek west, from Nauvoo to Salt Lake City, was featured on this program. Toward the end, it had portrayed young men and young women leaving from the airport in Salt Lake City to serve missions all around the world. For some unexplainable reason, this had brought him to tears. When he and I talked over breakfast that early July morning, Robin had not yet made the connection between that TV program and the Church of Jesus Christ of Latter-Day Saints. Only after he was baptized did he fully realize that the spirit had, in fact, touched him ten years before our meeting.

Our life together has been very different from our prior lives, where we each were busily engaged in raising young families. Only John lived with us now. At seventeen, my son stayed busy with high school and extracurricular activities. Ken was at ASU. Robin's youngest son, Aaron, was eight when we married. Because he lived out of state with his mother, he came to spend time with us only during his vacations. Robin's three older children attended college out of state.

Before my marriage to Robin, I had appealed to my children, explained to them that I would need their full cooperation. Without their help, my new marriage could not be fully successful. Of course, there were adjustments. Only weeks after returning from our London honeymoon, we arrived home after a pleasant evening out with friends. When the phone rang, my husband picked up the call. A police officer was holding John at the country club. He'd cornered my son with a beer can in his hand. Robin was already on his way out the door. Briefly I thought to stop him. Getting John should probably be my responsibility. When my husband and son returned, I told John we'd talk in the morning. In the privacy of our bedroom, I asked Robin what he'd said to John. His forthright response was, "What could I say? I was no different at that age." That is what I shared with my son the next morning, when John, in a rather defensive tone, approached me.

"So…what does Robin think of me now?"

What could have erupted into a family feud was quietly diffused by understanding and acceptance! I was beyond grateful. The developing relationships with each of our children has stayed courteous and respectful. With time, it has grown into genuine love.

Chapter 27

Our family has grown large. Over more than thirty years together, Robin and I have been blessed with many tender mercies. Our hearts are filled with gratitude and with love for each other and for our growing family. Writing my story has helped me cope and also begin to heal over the many months since John and Max also left us. I will always love them. Their lives mattered. Our departed loved ones live on still, just not with us. Their lives were destined for a different mission.

But if my loved ones had to go, I would want to have given my blessing. And deep in my heart I believe I did just that. Way back in the preexistence, there was a plan. I was part of this plan. I agreed to this plan, and now I'm living it. Throughout many difficult experiences in life, I have been blessed with a reassuring peace. The kind of peace that surpasses my understanding. How is it even possible that I can feel everything is okay? How is it possible that I can be happy, that I can feel joy?

My daughter-in-law, Cheryl, shared with me that the second year after their loss of John and Max was worse than the first. She struggled, as I have also struggled. From personal experience I know it takes a good two years to even feel like you can do this. That you can actually live this new life that so unexpectedly presented itself to you. In spite of everything, there is happiness and joy ahead. American philosopher and self-help author Wayne Dyer has stated, "With everything that has happened to you, you can either feel sorry for yourself, or treat what has happened as a gift. Everything is either an opportunity to grow, or an obstacle to keep you from growing. You get to choose."

Though pain has at times been exquisite, life has taught me to be thankful for difficult experiences and for knowledge gained through adversity. For I have not walked this difficult path of loss alone. I have come to know the love of my elder brother, Jesus Christ. This gift is available to each and all of God's children. Our Savior stands at the door and knocks. We get to choose if we will open our hearts and allow Him in. But only when our hearts are open can he permanently affect our lives. We can do hard things. And life can be good, even when it takes unexpected turns one never, ever wanted.

There was a time in my life when I was blindsided by choices made by some of my children. This caused me to question my own worth as a mother. And I asked my Heavenly Father, "Am I doing any good at all?" The answer came to me in a dream.

In my dream I approached a large gathering. People were eagerly crowding around something or someone. Curious to learn the reason for this gathering, I slowly made my way into the crowd. As I approached the center, I recognized to my astonishment that it was Christ whose presence was the reason for this momentous gathering. I do not recall seeing his face. But I felt his firm and loving embrace as he folded me into his arms. Never before, nor since, have I felt such deep and tender love. Like electricity, it surged through my body and soul while I rested myself in the embrace of my elder brother, my Savior and my Redeemer. It was a feeling of love so strong and pure and sweet that words are inadequate to truly convey how it affected my soul. With unquestionable certainty I knew that I was loved beyond measure. That Christ, indeed, knew who I was, and that I mattered to him and to my Heavenly Father. And I knew that my past efforts were completely and fully acceptable to them.

This dream has sustained me and given me reason to walk on with hope in my heart and with faith and acceptance of my Heavenly Father's plan. Even when I suffered the severe losses of my beloved family members. Even when my fervent prayers for my son John were not answered according to my own wishes. I know that Jesus Christ lives. He is the literal son of God. That same God who is our Eternal Father, the father of our spirits. It is he who gave his perfect son to succor us and to atone for our sins that we might also live again. I testify of the peace promised us in John 14:27: "Peace I leave with you, my peace I give unto you: not as the world giveth, give I unto you. Let not your heart be troubled, neither let it be afraid."

I have been blessed with His healing peace more often than I can count. Christ has walked with me through my challenges and through my deepest sorrows. His knowledge of pain and suffering is deeper and more profound than any of us can possibly experience. How he was able to endure the extreme agony of suffering the atonement is far beyond my limited understanding. But this I know: our redeemer wants each of us back. That is his mission, to bring us home. "For behold, this is my work and my glory—to bring to pass the immortality and eternal life of man" (Moses 1:39 in "The Pearl of Great Price").

Christ knows and loves each and every one of us individually. Many burdens in life are too heavy to carry. In various forms they come to most of us. My elder brother has carried my burdens—he has made them light. At times he has even carried me. He is our advocate with the Father. And we are cherished. As insufficient and imperfect as we mortals are, we are deeply cherished. There is no greater love than theirs.

Epilogue

Thanksgiving 2017 has come and gone with children and grandchildren visiting throughout the week. Already it is dark outside on this early Sunday evening in Chandler. This special week has culminated with the blessing of our twenty-fifth grandchild, Nicolas Alan Belnap, who is nearly six weeks old. A 1970 Beatles song, "Let It Be," is playing in our living room. My granddaughter Reagan is dancing to a video. Recital for Reagan's dance group is coming up in less than two weeks. My son John's eldest daughter has grown into a slender young girl of twelve.

My daughter-in-law has lingered. She leaves tomorrow morning with her three children. A nurse by profession, Cheryl is preparing to go back to work. Luke has a driver's permit. He will have a chance to practice his driving skills on their long drive to their new home in Utah, where they now live surrounded by Cheryl's large, close-knit family. Even at fifteen, Luke has shot to a height of six two, and he's still growing. A deep thinker, he's an exceptionally kind young man and an awesome big brother to his two younger sisters. Ashlynn's ninth birthday is coming up soon. As usual, she is full of energy. She and her sister are both in braces. They are sweet young girls. I am so grateful for the strength of these precious grandchildren and for their lovely mother.

As my beautiful young granddaughter dances so gracefully before me, I am struck by the lyrics to the Beatles song, "*Let it be.*" It felt right to *be still*.

To every person who has touched my life for good, I offer my deepest and most heartfelt gratitude. Daily, I thank my God that his goodness and mercy has followed me all the days of my life.

It has taken longer to finish my story than ever anticipated. It was mid-July in 2016 when I started writing. Today is Monday, April 27, 2020, my angel grandson's twenty-first birthday. On that special Tuesday in 1999, Cheryl so graciously invited me to be with her and John in the delivery room for the birth of their firstborn. I am eternally grateful for this most special gift. The life of my grandson Max and the life of each of our loved ones who have gone before us is a cherished memory. We never forget.

About the Author

Karin Larsen Ford spent her early years in Czechoslovakia before moving to her father's country, Denmark, with her family after WWII. At nineteen, she came to California, where she eventually married and started her family. A retired dental hygienist, Karin holds a bachelor of science from the University of St. Francis in Joliet, Illinois. She currently lives in St. George, Utah, with her husband, Robin. Together they enjoy exploring the colorful vistas and rugged beauty of southern Utah.

CPSIA information can be obtained
at www.ICGtesting.com
Printed in the USA
FSHW010231151021
85461FS